# THE MANAGEMENT RIGHTS FORMULA

## Work Smarter, Create Wealth
*and*
## Live the Lifestyle You Deserve

### JESSICA DONG

Disclaimer

All the information, techniques, skills and concepts contained within this publication are of the nature of general comment only and are not in any way recommended as individual advice. The intent is to offer a variety of information to provide a wider range of choices now and in the future, recognising that we all have widely diverse circumstances and viewpoints. Should any reader choose to make use of the information contained herein, this is their decision, and the contributors (and their companies), authors and publishers do not assume any responsibilities whatsoever under any condition or circumstances. It is recommended that the reader obtain their own independent advice.

First Edition 2019

Copyright © 2019 by Jessica Dong

All rights reserved. No part of this publication may be reproduced, stored in a retrieval system, or transmitted in any form or by any means, electronic, mechanical, photocopying, recording or otherwise, without the prior written permission from Jessica Dong.

A catalogue record for this book is available from the National Library of Australia

Cataloguing-in-Publication entry: Dong, Jessica
Management Rights Formula: Work Smarter, Create Wealth and Live The Lifestyle You Deserve. /Jessica Dong
1st ed.

ISBN: 9780648427896 (pbk)

Business -- Australia
Finance, Personal --Australia.
332.63240994

*Try not to become a man of success. But rather try to become a man of value.*
**~Albert Einstein**

# TESTIMONIALS

Jessica is an expert in management rights. She took the time and had the patience to help me pick out the perfect business for me. SIRE's service and products are top notch. I came away completely happy and satisfied.

— **Jimmy Yan**, Founder of VITO 888 Pty Ltd

It was a great pleasure getting to know Jessica and the SIRE Team. I'm relatively new to this industry, and Jessica was helpful and enthusiastic, providing tips and answering all my questions. And after I signed the contract, she helped make the transition to the final settlement a smooth one. I would highly recommend SIRE Management Rights to anyone who is interested in having a future career in the industry.

— **Charles Chiu**, Founder of Neon Life Pty Ltd

I met Jess and Richard few years ago when I bought my first management rights business. They are trustworthy and warm-hearted and not like other agents who try and push the buyer. They make sure to help every customer on the basis of fairness and honesty. This is the main reason I chose them to be my second MR business purchasing agent. I would recommend SIRE to newbies who don't have much experience and knowledge regarding the MR business. SIRE knows what a buyer needs. Their experienced staff assists buyers from day one, all the way through to post-settlement. Contact the SIRE Team and experience the SIRE difference.

— **Chris Li**, Founder and Director of CJE Pty Ltd QLD.

After trying many other agents, I went to Jessica who understood my needs. Not only can she help the novice to fully understand the body corporate interview process, but she also helps lay the foundation for the operation after settlement. I'm grateful to Jessica and SIRE Management Rights for their help.

— **Hong Chen**, Founder of RH&L Pty Ltd QLD

SIRE Management Rights has rich industry experience in management rights, and their active and responsible attitude is remarkable. SIRE Management Rights provides an efficient communication bridge for buyers and sellers from day one, and the exclusive SIRE Body Corporate Interview Workshop is an extraordinary add-on benefit to buyers and sellers. I would recommend SIRE Management Rights to anyone thinking about selling their business.

— **Sam Huang**, Director JH Pro Management Pty Ltd

Jessica helped me find a buyer for my business within two weeks. The sale of management right it is a complicated process. We really needed someone kind and patient who could walk us through the process. If you want to buy or sell a management rights, you need to contact SIRE Management Rights.

— **Bruce Huang**, Connect Education Network Pty. Ltd.

The SIRE Team was knowledgeable and understanding and had total confidence that they would find the right buyer for my business at an excellent price, Their knowledge and assistance was invaluable to me. I have discovered the benefit of selling a management rights business and

will definitely be using the SIRE Team for all future transactions, as well as referring them to anyone I know who is selling their management rights.
— **Derek Edgar**, K4 Property Management

The selling of management rights is complex and requires diligent work and specialised skills in the management rights field. SIRE Management Rights' system and process gave me peace of mind. The body corporate interview training is dynamic, unique, practical and up-to date. I would highly recommend SIRE Management Rights to anyone who is thinking of selling or buying management rights.
— **Simon Tang**, Founder, Kenon Group Pty Ltd

Jessica is legendary in the management rights business. The SIRE Team understood what had to be done and got on with it. I would recommend SIRE Management Rights to buyers and sellers.
— **Tim Wright**, Director Australian Rental Management Pty Ltd QLD

After going to other brokers with disastrous results, Jessica and The SIRE Team brought us buyers who really wanted our business. Jessica is great at talking with both parties to negotiate and reach a win-win outcome. I recommend the SIRE Team to anyone buying or selling management rights.
— **Jiang Ping**, Director AUCN Pty Ltd QLD

When we came to SIRE, we were concerned we couldn't get the asking price in the short time frame we needed to sell our management rights, due to other business commitments. We chose Jessica, because of her efficiency and unique approach working with prospective buyers. We would recommend Jessica and SIRE Management Rights to anyone who needs to sell or buy a management rights business.
— **Taurus Yang**, Founder of The Yang Circle Pty Ltd QLD

After finding it difficult to run several sites, we decided to sell our Sherwood businesses. SIRE's innovative marketing initiatives led to more viewings by potential buyers. We have no reservation recommending SIRE to anyone who would like to sell their management rights businesses.

— **Leo Ho**, Director of LJ Ho Pty Ltd QLD

When we considered selling our management rights, I called Jessica to help me get my documentation organized and guide us through the sale process. Jessica and the SIRE Team are efficient and always love to help. They provide lots of useful information and advice. They helped us find qualified buyers and submitted several good offers to us within two weeks. The whole process was easy and simple, and more importantly, we got the price we wanted. We really appreciated Jessica and The SIRE Team's excellent work and would highly recommend them to anyone buying or selling a management rights business.

— **Philip Li and Jessica Chen**, Managing Director
– AFX Management Pty Ltd QLD

# DEDICATION

It's truly a team effort to write and produce this book, and it would not exist without the support of the contributing authors, management rights owners and industry partners.

I'd like to take this opportunity to thank you all. We share the vision to inspire and influence change and have a positive impact on the strata hotels, motels and accommodation industry as a whole.

The secret to any successful venture is seeking out those who've prospered, and learning from them. By sharing your knowledge, you're helping others to follow in your footsteps.

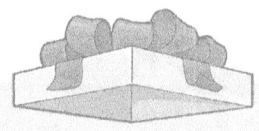

# THE MANAGEMENT RIGHTS FORMULA BONUS GIFTS

Simply by purchasing a copy of *The Management Rights Formula*, you now have access to a range of incredible gifts that will increase your income, so you can build a more valuable management rights business.

By putting together the most inspiring people in the industry who are willing to spill their secrets, we are giving you the tools to go above and beyond what you ever thought possible.

We can't possibly include all of their incredible knowledge in one book, so we've created a special website that has loads of extra goodies just for you that will keep you motivated on your journey to success.

We at *The Management Rights Formula* Headquarters like to keep up-to-date with technology, so you can have quicker and easier access to the information you'll need on your path to success.

These free gifts are located throughout the book at the end of each chapter and can be accessed all in one place on our dedicated website, **www.mrformula.com.au**.

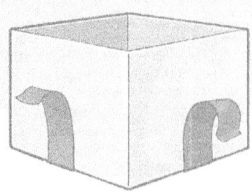

# ACKNOWLEDGEMENTS

*To my children, James and Victor, who are my angels! You're both so caring and fun to be around. You teach me something new every day☺. I write to record the life experiences your father and I have journeyed through before and after you were born, to set a good example for you.*

*To my husband, love and best mate, Richard, who has always supported me since we were rebel teenagers with ambition. Thank you for your support, ideas, execution and big, kind heart filled with unconditional love.*

*To all the contributing authors: This has been incredibly humbling. I'm in awe of your commitment and generosity in sharing your experience, knowledge and insights. You're truly inspirational.*

*To all our vendors who trusted The SIRE Team with their biggest asset, we say, "Thank you". As you ride off into the sunset on a yacht to travel around the world and follow your passions, we feel a great sense of fulfilments and contribution.*

*To our buyers who trusted us with their life savings and invested in the wonderful management rights industry, we feel great joy and inspiration seeing you grow, prosper and become movers and shakers!*

# CONTENTS

Introduction — xv
by Jessica Dong

The Experts — 1

## CHAPTER ONE — 3
**Jessica Dong**
Let's Buy Management Rights: A Simplified Science

## CHAPTER TWO — 27
**Danny Little**
The Winning Formula: The 3E's

## CHAPTER THREE — 45
**Jason Fu**
Show Me the Money: What You Need to Know to Succeed

## CHAPTER FOUR — 73
**Michael Joseph O'Farrell**
Break Through Your First Million, Systemise, Build a Team and Increase Your Profit

## CHAPTER FIVE                           93
### Sylvia Johnston
Turbo Charge Your Profit: Make Your Technology Work for You

## CHAPTER SIX                             121
### John Mahoney
Prevent Forest Fires: Strategic Legal Advice from Business-Minded Lawyers

## CHAPTER SEVEN                        147
### Scott Lai, CPA
Keep What You Make: Asset Protection and Smart Tax Strategies

## CHAPTER EIGHT                         163
### Richard Skiba & Jessica Dong
Management Rights Super Exit Strategy: The Fast and Simple Way to Sell Your Business at the Highest Price

## HOW TO CLAIM YOUR FREE BONUS GIFTS                199

# INTRODUCTION

by Jessica Dong

In 2015, our company had just settled a portfolio of buildings and complexes, completing a great year.

One beautiful Brisbane morning at 5:30 am, I was getting ready for a quick gym session, when I checked my phone and saw eight missed calls from our manager, Daniel. He'd been in an accident and had spent the night in emergency. Daniel is our general manager. He's the one who knows everything about the buildings in our portfolio. He's efficient, experienced, hard-working and amiable, with a laid-back personality. In other words, he's a star. Let me put it this way: he's so good at what he does, that at the time our business couldn't run without him.

Long story short, we quickly found an experienced manager named Debra. She was stylish, friendly and has a beautiful soul. Everyone loved Deb. Since she had over ten years of experience in management rights and good references from her previous owners and clients, we assumed she understood management rights and would be great at assisting in the handling of our portfolios, but nothing could be further from the truth.

Every building is different, and every team member has their own style. The harsh reality is that managing one building by yourself is quite different from managing a portfolio of buildings and adapting to a team in which everyone uses a different system.

There was a communication breakdown, and we were putting out fires while desperately trying to stay on top of what was going on. As the week progressed, three of us were stressing out and becoming impatient with each other and our contractors. After a week, complaints started coming in.

This was a huge wake-up call to me that being a good manager doesn't mean you can be a good business owner. It also taught me that a business can't rely on one person. At that point, I knew I needed to change my way of doing things before I ended up disappointing our owners and losing my life savings.

I decided we needed to get some help from a successful on-site manager who handled multiple big buildings, whose owners loved him and yet still has time for the finer things in life.

I registered for a business systemising free event. When I told them my situation, they recommended we build a real system that didn't rely on one person who, if he left the company, would cause the whole business to collapse.

I then signed up for a workshop that assisted business owners who were overworked and burnt out. They taught us how to improve efficiency, systemise processes and procedures, create video training and utilise new technologies to do all the heavy lifting in order to get the work done in half the time.

What I discovered was that we weren't lacking information or strategies, we just needed the ability to take action. We had to figure out the best way to do everything, from creating easy-to-follow training videos all the way down to the correct formula for the cleaning fluid used to mop the floors.

Once we learned how to use the tools, which took just ten minutes, we were able to produce how-to videos. Then we made sure that any staff member who had the log-in could search the videos and be trained in exactly the same way to consistently produce high-quality results.

Now it doesn't matter if our best employee can't make it into work. We can quickly train up staff in a week, and the best part of all is that I don't even need to do it myself. This process allows us to take on new buildings and ensure we have adequate human resources to look after the owners and buildings.

I also learned that there's a system and a formula for everything you want to achieve. And it's much better to emulate what works from the people who walked the same road rather than wasting vast amounts of time on trial and error.

The tried and tested system is also useful for single operators in a smaller complex or building. By implementing new technology and strategies, you can get all the work done in half the time, so you're able to work on your business and increase income or do the things you enjoy. By systemising your processes and procedures, you can train a relief manager to deliver the exact same result for your owners without you personally training them or having to be there while you're on holidays.

My promise to you is that by reading this book, even if it's just one page a day, you'll pick up the mindset, ideas, tools and action steps, to buy management rights at a great price, operate efficiently, grow your income and live the lifestyle you desire.

Then, when you're ready to sell, the SIRE Team will be able to get you the highest price for your business.

> *The Management Rights Formula transforms self-employed on-site managers into systemised business owners who take daily meaningful, impactful actions to produce desired results.*
> **~Jessica Dong**

# THE EXPERTS

In the following chapters, experts in the field of management rights share their experiences, stories, tips and tools that will make the process of finding the appropriate management rights opportunity a simple and smooth one. By utilizing these strategies, you'll be able to settle into your business, improve the efficiency of your operations, build a team around you and maximise your income.

You'll build a legacy management rights business that enhances the experiences of your owners, guests and residents. And when it's time to exit, you will have a highly desirable management rights business that commands top offers.

> *By the end of this book, I hope to provide you with some new inspirational ideas and initiatives that will motivate you to take action, so you can move one step closer to your freedom!*
> **~Jessica Dong**
> SIRE Management Rights QLD

# CHAPTER ONE

# Jessica Dong

## Let's Buy Management Rights: A Simplified Science

> *Work, love and play are the great balance wheels of one's being.*
> **~Orison Swett Marden**
> Founder of *Success* magazine

Jessica Dong is a management rights sales specialist and co-founder of SIRE, a company that specialises in management rights and strata hotel/motel sales.

Through her company, Jessica has helped hundreds of people find the best management rights to suit their needs so they can live a life filled with purpose, secure income, and free time to do what they love. The SIRE Team transforms management rights newbies into super on-site managers, who everyone, from residents and guests to the body corporate, absolutely love.

Six years ago, Jessica:
- didn't have enough time to look after her young son and baby
- had to travel overseas once a week to get a pay cheque that hardly covered her increasing expenses
- was rapidly running out of equity due to increased expenses and less time to work
- was overwhelmed and directionless.

But her life changed when she discovered that climbing the corporate ladder didn't give her much time to take care of her family, so she took a vital step and got into the management rights industry. Now she works from home and sets her own hours. Her wonderful clients and mentors inspire her every day to improve her efficiency and implement new strategies to secure a stable cash flow, as well as help other managers and operators optimise their business and maximise income.

Today, Jessica directly impacts the lives of accommodation and management rights owners. A cross between a strategist and sales specialist, Jessica is as comfortable working with mum and dad operators as she is with hotel chains, developers and new entries to the industry. She also loves sharing her knowledge with others and keeps herself busy with public speaking.

By using their systemised and simple process, Jessica and the entire SIRE team, help buyers purchase suitable management rights, operate well and build wealth.

*" The real goal of what we're doing is to have a positive impact on the community in which we live, and that means starting with the buildings we manage and care for."*
~**Jessica Dong**
SIRE Management Rights

## What does 'The Management Rights Formula' mean?

During my many years in the industry, I've had the privilege of interviewing various management rights owners and their team members, most of whom truly know how to optimise the operation of their business and have their team perform like a well-oiled machine. All of this is underpinned by a clear vision, good planning and systemised processes and procedures, as well as strategic delegation that gives business owners the time to focus on improving the building and getting a good return on their investment.

I call these dedicated people 'management rights insiders'. Because they've generously shared their tips, experiences and strategies with me, I'm able to pass this information on to experienced and new managers. And in turn, they can purchase the best management rights for themselves and make the most of their experience once they settle in.

However, knowledge without action is meaningless, so it's important to follow a proven formula and take action on it to get the desired result. And you must systemise the process to deliver that result consistently. Whether you're the one taking on the task or delegating it, there needs to be continuous learning, the willingness to take action and the ability to measure and improve your business operations. Whether it's in marketing, sales, procurement or service delivery, by following the right formula, you'll be able to deliver the best outcome in the most efficient way.

Give yourself permission to live the lifestyle you deserve. Buy the right business and build it up, so you can create wealth and change lives in the process.

> *There are essentially two things that will make you wiser: the books you read and the people you meet.*
> ~Charles "Tremendous" Jones

**Why did you choose management rights as a profession?**
Nineteen years ago, I read *Rich Dad, Poor Dad* by Robert T. Kiyosaki while trying to figure out what I should do with my life after university, apart from getting a nine-to-five job and living pay cheque to pay cheque.

While I was focused on my goals and career, I was unable to allocate enough time and money to bond with my family and friends. It soon became clear to me that I should be working toward investing into my own business that would generate money, even if I wasn't physically present.

Ten years ago, I made a decision to do something about it. I used the equity in two of my properties and channelled it into my own management rights business. I read everything on the subject, including information about the body corporate, caretaking, building management, sales, relationship building, communications and systems.

I was also mentored by some of the most successful management rights insiders, and more importantly, applied everything they taught me into building a comfortable income and lifestyle. This experience made me realise management rights was the best business vehicle to provide me with cash flow and flexible time, particularly considering I'm very conservative with my money and don't like taking risks.

**You've been selling management rights for six years now. How do you feel about the industry?**

I love the management rights industry because of all the benefits I've already mentioned. The sky's the limit. I meet wonderful people and learn something new every day. I rarely have the same experience twice. The fuel for the management rights vehicle is efficiency and productivity, which makes it go faster and perform better.

You get rewarded by delivering better value to your owners, while also having more free time and income. Many of my clients have benefited from my personal experience in building management, as well as the practical and valuable education I share from management rights insiders regarding the improvement and efficiency of their operations.

**What is management rights?**

Around fifty years ago, the first management rights (MR) business emerged on the Gold Coast in QLD Australia. Since then, it's become extremely popular, as it offers the owners of strata buildings (properties that are adjoined, such as apartments or townhouses) great benefits and services.

There are three components to management rights: a manager's unit, a caretaking agreement and a letting agreement. The on-site manager is also called the resident letting agent and usually owns and lives in the manager's unit, getting paid a salary to maintain the complex, as well as paid commission to rent out the units. Because they're not only part owners of the building, but also live and work on the property, the manager is motivated to provide top-notch, value-added services to the body corporate (the collective body of owners within the complex, building owners, residents and guests).

From a business point of view, management rights has a built-in niche, because all the services are located in the one building.

> *Unity is strength...when there is teamwork and collaboration, wonderful things can be achieved.*
> ~Matte J.T. Stepanek

**How many different types of management rights are there?**
SIRE Management Rights mainly sells six types of management rights, where the duties are specified in the caretaking agreement, and the differences are in the letting part of the business:

- **Permanent management rights**
  Offers a six-month (or longer) lease to the rental market for long-term accommodation.
- **Holiday management rights**
  Offers anything from one night to three-month stays for people on holiday.
- **Mixed management rights**
  Offers permanent and holiday lettings.
- **Student management rights**
  Provides accommodation to students. This is for buildings located next to universities and other educational providers.
- **Corporate management rights**
  Provides accommodation to business travellers when they require less than a three-month accommodation or prefer not to sign a lease

- **Aged care management rights**
  Provides four different levels of care and accommodation to over fifty residents.

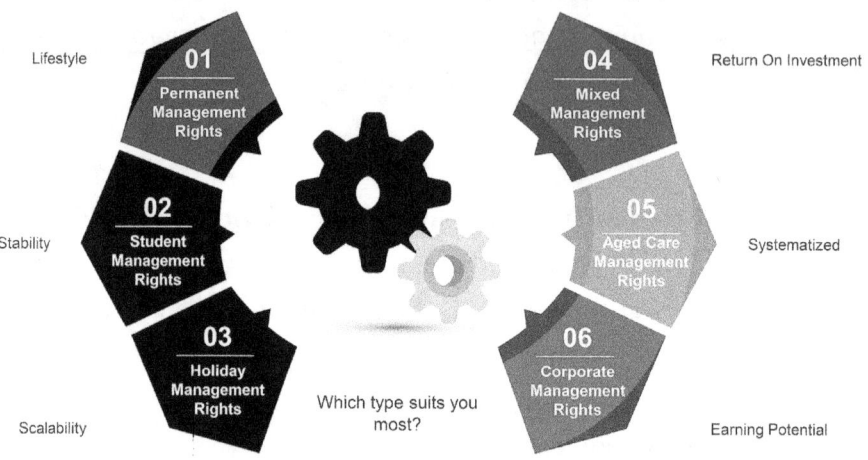

The best way to understand each style of management rights is to join a SIRE management rights inspection. Please visit **www.mrformula.com.au/buy.html** to register for an on-site inspection where the SIRE Team and manager will go through all the nuts and bolts with you.

**What are the income streams for management rights owners?**
There are many sources of income for the management right owner, with the two major ones being the body corporate salary and letting commissions/fees.

A body corporate salary applies to all different types of management rights. Within the caretaking agreement, there's a specified annually increasing amount of remuneration for the duties performed to maintain the common area and facilities.

Management rights owners also offer letting services to investor owners. For this they receive a letting fee, which is a one-off payment made at the start of a new tenancy agreement. It usually comes out of the first rent payment and covers the cost of advertising the property and setting up the tenancy agreement with the new tenant. In addition, they receive a letting commission, which is ongoing.

For different types of management rights, there are many other sources of income, such as providing repair and maintenance services for the owners, cleaning services for the residences and commissions received from touring companies. For strata hotels and motels with restaurants and bars, income can be generated from these sources as well. Over the years, we've compiled a list of over twenty ways management rights insiders can increase their income. You can download this list on our website, at **www.mrformula.com.au/increase-income.html**.

## What are some of the reasons people buy management rights?

Here are some of the responses I've received when I ask people why they buy management rights:

- I'm planning on having baby this year, and I want to work from home and look after my family.
- I was just made redundant and want to be my own boss this time around.
- I want to work my own hours.
- I need a stable income.
- I want a low-risk business.
- I'd like to invest in something that has an established, time-tested business model.

- I'm looking for a business that provides the highest leverage using the bank's money.
- I'm interested in a business that's easy to operate.
- I want a business that has a clear, easy and profitable exit strategy.

What they find is that management rights is the only business that ticks all the boxes for them.

**What's the most important step in buying a suitable management rights?**
The type of management rights you decide to purchase must be aligned with why you want to own this business. First, you need to be clear with your vision: the clearer the picture, the fewer the choices and the easier the decision.

To clarify your WHY, please go to **www.mrformula.com.au/why**.

Once there, use the *clearer vision formula* to help you narrow down what type of management rights aligns with your goals. Figuring out your WHY will get you to where you want to go faster and more efficiently.

> *Well done is better than well said.*
> ~**Benjamin Franklin**

### What are the financial considerations regarding purchasing a management rights?
The best thing about management rights is its lending potential. Banks can lend up to 70 percent of the whole purchase price, which really demonstrates the stability of this type of business.

If you want to find out your price range, please fill out the *Use Other People's Money* questionnaire online at **www.mrformula.com.au/opm.html**, and a management rights specialised finance broker will call to assist you with determining your price range.

**How does someone identify which management rights business they should choose?**
This is a question I get asked all the time. Some buyers tell me they want a management rights that generates big income, has a low multiplier, requires minimal workload, has a long agreement and the manager's unit has a low price tag, but they need it to be spacious and in a great location.

Let me be real: this type of business doesn't exist. It's like when you're buying a house, and you're on a limited budget, but you want it to be a mansion in the richest area.

I've also worked with buyers who ask for every single listing's full details, including an information memorandum, a profit-and-loss statement and agreements, but never attend any inspections. Then they wonder after two years why they haven't found anything. Coming to our inspections is the best way to find a suitable business in the quickest time possible.

Every member of the SIRE Team is an expert in management rights and follows the Management Rights Formula. We've all been through the buying and selling process ourselves, so we can share the mistakes we've made, as well as our experience and knowledge, which will save you time and money.

If you're new to the industry, you'll learn to identify the pros and cons of each business and the right tools to improve it and increase income, just by talking with the SIRE team during the inspection. For instance, something you might view as a negative on paper, when you bring it up during the inspection, we might be able to shed a different light on it, which in turn can become a great opportunity for you.

If you're interested in some real case studies, you can also attend our monthly FREE information event by registering at **www.siremanagemnetrights.com.au/freevent.html**.

> *Ninety-five percent of success is just showing up.*
> **~Woody Allen**

### How can someone ensure they don't miss out on an excellent management rights opportunity?

Once you're clear on why you're buying a management rights, and what your price range is, you need to attend some SIRE inspections. When you see a management rights that meets your requirements, you'll be able to identify it right away. But you need to be quick, as most good listings receive multiple offers.

Our offer form is designed to ensure your interest is protected. This means you will be subjected to financial verification, legal due diligence and financial approval, so at any stage if something isn't quite right, the SIRE team will assist both parties in reaching an amicable agreement. Rest assured that you're totally protected during this process.

## Once they've made the decision, how should they calculate what to offer?

What to offer is always case by case.

The price of a management rights business is usually the value of the manager's unit, plus the cost of the actual business. It's valued and sold using a 'multiplier' of annual net income or profit, which is the year's net return, times what the buyer will pay the seller. It's all about supply and demand.

The size of the multiplier is contingent upon market conditions, which includes the influence of banks and other valuers, and can depend on variables like location, age and size of the property, market demand and occupancy, and interest rates.

With so many variables, it's unlikely any two management rights transactions will ever be the same. What this means is that in management rights, you're really buying the security of a future income stream. The more work or risk involved in the investment, the higher the return you can expect. A low-risk, low-effort investment in a building with a twenty-five-year agreement might command a six or even higher multiplier, whereas a business subject to market fluctuations might have a 3.5 or lower multiplier.

If you're a management rights buyer using cash, and you want a 20 percent return on the business part of the investment, to find out what you'll pay, multiply the net return per annum by one hundred and divide by twenty. So if the business nets $100,000 per annum, you'll calculate the price like this:

$$100{,}000 \times 100 \text{ divided by } 20 = \$500{,}000$$

What this translates to is $100,000, or a 20 percent return, for a $500,000 business.

The way you get the multiplier is to divide twenty into one hundred, which equals five. So the new calculation is the multiplier times the net return, or:

$$\$100{,}000 \times 5 = \$500{,}000$$

This means it's important to work with someone who really understands you, your vision and your business module. For instance, if one buyer owns five buildings in the area, the SIRE team can save them a lot of time and money by showing them another business with a much more efficient system in place that can be implemented across the whole portfolio to improve the overall performance. We share the true value of the management rights, while also letting you know how to overcome any perceived flaws. This kind of valuable information is why buyers continue to utilise SIRE's services year after year.

### How much should someone offer for the manager's unit?
One of the reasons people love management rights is because they get to work from home.

The manager's unit is the only place where you can operate the letting business, so therefore there's no comparison with the other units in the building or complex. This means it needs to be compared with the manager's units in nearby complexes. Typically, if the unit is similar to others in a similar complex or building, then the price should be at least 10 percent more. Most of the manager's units come with an office on title and exclusive use of areas in the complex. All of this should be considered during the bank valuation process.

**What else needs to be considered before and after signing the contract?**
I've sold lots of great management rights over the years and always get multiple offers. This means many people do miss out, even though they might have been just as qualified as the other buyers.

What I've found is that the reason they were unable to take advantage of a fantastic opportunity is because they were unprepared. To save you time, I'd like to offer suggestions as to the key areas in which you need to get organised.

1. **Get financial pre-approval.**
   You must use finance brokers who are specialised in management rights to assist you in working out your ideal price range.

2. **Set up your purchasing structure.**
   Many buyers use a company and family trust to purchase the management rights. Both provide tax benefits and risk protection.

3. **Get an RLA license**
   You'll need a Resident Letting Agent (RLA) license if you're going to live on-site, or a full license if you're thinking of owning multiple complexes/buildings and intend to have staff live on-site.

4. **Get some experience in the industry.**
   We're always happy to assist you in getting hands-on experience. Just email me at **sales@siremanagementrights.com.au** with your CV, and we can get that arranged.

Once you've completed all of these steps and you make an offer, the vendor will definitely take yours more seriously and consider it first. This puts you in an excellent position to go to the top of the list and beat out the competition.

You can find everything you need in the resource session in the back of this book.

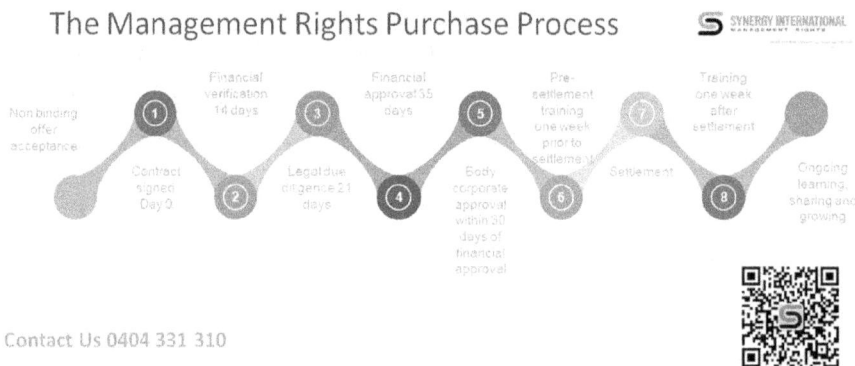

## Why should someone work with management rights professionals during the contract process?

Management rights is a specialised industry, and not many people understand it. Even today, we witness many developers making mistakes in setting up the agreement, so the management rights of a perfect building/complex ends up being unsaleable.

Over the years, I've come across buyers who use a solicitor, accountant, real estate agent or financier to assist with the process, but none of them are specialised in management rights, so they end up wasting lots of money and time. There are quite a few hoops to jump through between the contract signing to settlement, and if you don't have someone with years of industry experience on your side, you won't know how to deal with the potential problems that could arise during the process.

The industry is also changing all the time, so unless you're living and breathing management rights, you probably won't know how to identify and get around potential issues and solve challenges as they come up. By associating yourself with any of the professionals included in this book, I guarantee you'll come out on top.

One of our proudest achievements at SIRE Management Rights is that we have a 100 percent body corporate approval rating. If you would like to know more about the body corporate interview process, please visit **www.mrformula.com.au/interview.html** and attend our monthly interview information session.

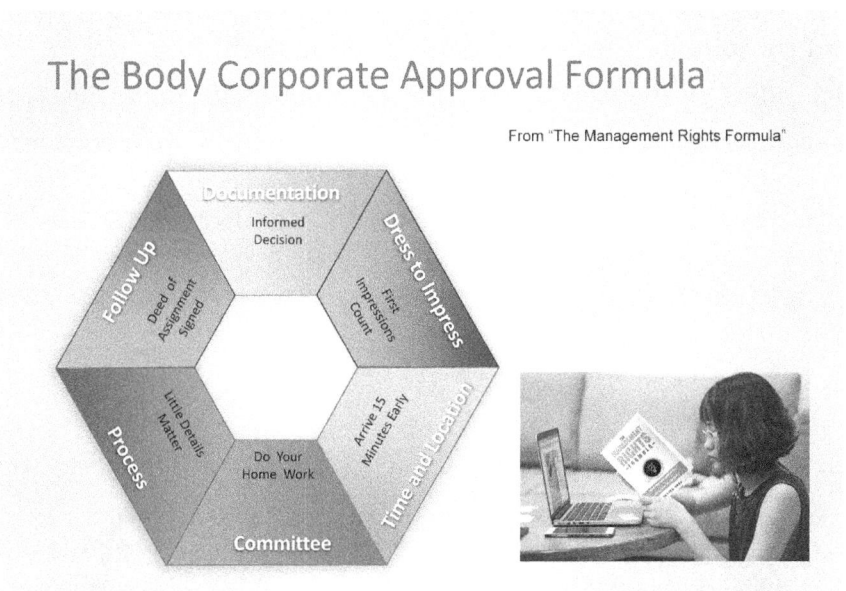

## How does someone prepare for the settlement process?

Once you've received financial approval, there are still many steps you need to go through before the process is complete, such as the body corporate interview preparation, the actual interview, attending training with the out-going manager, setting up the advertising platform and the software handover.

Once the settlement occurs, some new managers overlook the importance of establishing a professional working relationship from day one with the body corporate, committee members, owners and body corporate manager. Since this is the take-off phase of your flight that will help make the rest of your trip cruise along, it would be a mistake to neglect it. All management rights insiders follow a formula that we can share with you in our monthly interview information session.

## How long does it take to settle into a new management rights and consolidate your relationship and income?

Depending on the size of your building/complex, it would take six to twelve months. The next step would then be to improve your efficiency.

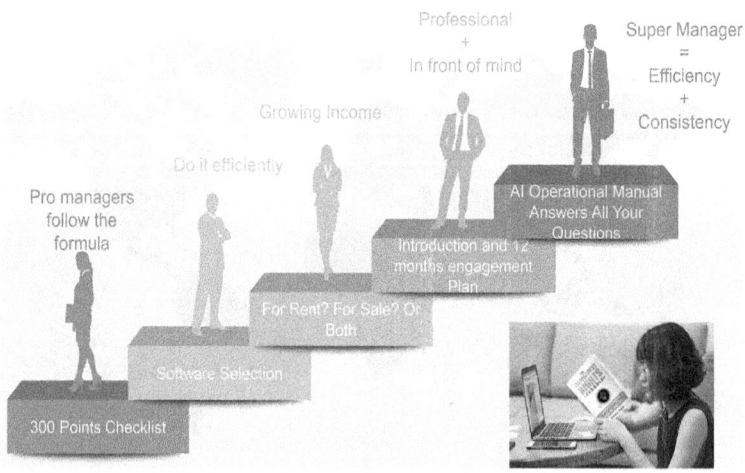

**How many steps are there to go from newbie to competent on-site manager?**

There are five simple steps:

1. Clarify your desired lifestyle, income and level of freedom, and then write down your WHY and share it with The SIRE Team. We will support you along the way.

2. Attend inspections with The SIRE Team to discover the true value of each management rights.

3. Associate yourself with management rights insiders, and take impactful action by following the Management Rights Formula.

4. To ensure a smooth transition, sign a well-planned contract.

5. Use the time from contract date to settlement to fully prepare yourself. Going through a well-structured process ensures an excellent take off to your new management rights career. Then you can work on your business daily to improve efficiency and income.

Enjoy the process, and set aside some time each week to attend our inspections. Then email me your questions, and share what you liked and didn't like. The SIRE team will be glad to show you a management right that meets your requirements.

Please feel free to share this information with your friends, and of course if they would like to get into management rights, please invite them to one of our inspections.

## What action steps would you recommend for someone who wants to buy management rights?

1.  Make a list of your desired requirements from the purchase of your management rights

    **Example One: Single Operator**
    Income: $150,000
    Location: Between Gold Coast and Brisbane, with an easy drive for partner to get to work.
    Manager unit: three bedrooms (or more)
    Lifestyle: Set own hours, more gardening, less cleaning.
    Growth potential: Doesn't matter. A stable cash flow is the goal.

    **Example Two: Husband and Wife Operators**
    Income: $300,000+
    Location: Brisbane or Gold Coast
    Manager unit: One to three bedrooms, so there's enough room for staff.
    Lifestyle: Set own hours. Have the staff do most of the work.
    Growth potential: Low occupancy rate. Rundown business/building that can be refurbished.

    **Example Three: Company/Investor Operator**
    Income: $1,000,000+
    Location: QLD
    Manager unit: For staff only.
    Lifestyle: Set own hours. Have staff do most of the work.
    Growth potential: Building can be refurbished. Improve OTA booking, direct booking, etc.

2. Get started.
   - Register for the Management Rights Formula information session.
   - Email your requirements to SIRE Management Rights.
   - Book three inspections and schedule in your diary.
   - Record your own action plan.

**DO IT NOW!** It's your turn to make a list of what you want as a result of buying a management rights business.

Income:
_____

Location:
_____

Manager unit:
_____

Lifestyle:
_____

Growth potential:
_____

Other:
_____

Three jumpstart actions:

1.
_____

2.
_____

3.
_____

Start Date:
_____

## The seven wisdoms from this chapter:

1. Be specific and flexible as to the lifestyle and management rights you desire.

2. Identify those who have achieved success, mingle with them and follow their formula.

3. The four major reasons to get into management rights are:
   - stable cash flow
   - flexible working hours
   - the ability to leverage other people's money
   - the potential to grow an assert to create wealth.

4. By failing to prepare for your body corporate interview, you're setting yourself up for failure.

5. Energies are contagious. Surround yourself with people who are experts in the management rights industry.

6. When building your team, only use specialists in management rights, which includes:
   - the SIRE Team
   - a solicitor
   - an accountant
   - a financier
   - Management Rights Formula insiders.

7. The great aim of education isn't knowledge, but acting on that knowledge.

## Special Offer for *The Management Rights Formula* Readers

We're offering an extraordinary opportunity to participate in our exclusive three-hour workshop, entitled *Apply the Management Rights Formula*, where some of the most successful insiders share everything you need to know about acquiring an excellent management rights, so you can live the lifestyle you deserve.

You'll learn their strategies, processes, systems and procedures for building better relationships with owners and improving the products and services you provide to the market, so you can deliver the performance your owners will rave about.

This event runs the first Wednesday of each month at seven p.m., but we only have space available for twenty people, so book your seat today.

Please note that attendance will be on a first come, first served basis, as we believe this is the fairest way to allocate the limited number of spots we have available for this FREE event. Go to **www.mrformula.com.au/bonus** to start your adventure today.

# CHAPTER TWO
# Danny Little

## The Winning Formula: The 3E's

*" Excellence is not a skill, it's an attitude."*
~Ralph Marston

Danny Little has always lived his life by the three "E" rule:

- Enthusiasm
- Energy
- Excellence

After twenty-four years in retailing, in which he won the Junior Retailer of the Year Queensland, oversaw the major expansion of twelve stores and twice won the prestigious Target Merchandising Award for innovation and excellence, he decided to go into business for himself and chose management rights. Following some early successes, he formed Bluechip Resorts and began an expansion program where he became part or full owner of thirteen buildings. During this time he managed permanent, holiday, student and corporate buildings throughout Queensland.

In 2012, he began MRAS Consulting, which now provides a diverse range of services, including management training, business coaching, design and operational assistance, remuneration assessments and common property assessments.

He's assisted clients in China, Singapore, Kuala Lumpur and the Philippines, and is often requested by industry associations and experts to help new entrants in the management right industry understand the Australian business landscape and what the management rights industry is all about.

## Why did you become a management rights owner?

Following a successful retailing career, in which I became the Queensland Sales and Marketing Manager for all the Target retail stores from Darwin to Coffs Harbour, I made the decision to go into business for myself.

After many years in the corporate world, I was excited by the challenge of running my own business and being rewarded for those efforts. It became an overwhelming ambition.

## How did you get started?

As with many people who decide to enter our industry, I tried to get as much information on what management rights could offer and how to go about starting the process. In the early days of 1999, there weren't a lot of associations or trainers that could help you through the journey. Much of the legwork was done on my own through due diligence.

The way I do most things in life is that I review as many different options as possible, so I started by going on several property inspections to fully understand the number of opportunities available within the industry.

## What steps did you take to start your first management rights??

I'd worked with a close friend who'd left Target four years earlier and had created a successful business selling management rights. I did several inspections with him and spent a great deal of time understanding what had to be done to get into the industry.

Some of the best advice I received was to surround myself with experts. My lawyer of nearly nineteen years is still my lawyer today, and the industry has now grown to the point that there are several professional law firms specialising in the management rights industry.

Once I'd selected the type of business I wanted, I was guided by industry professionals to ensure that the journey was as smooth as it could be.

**How do you go from a concept or idea to being able to implement it into your business?**
My whole working life had been about *systems and procedures*. One of the great benefits of working with highly disciplined retailers is that it provides you with a wonderful grounding for this industry. Customer service, reporting, presentation and discipline, as well as a sense of routine, were the skills we utilised to establish ourselves in the industry. Having a strong marketing background was also advantageous, as the industry hadn't matured yet to the number of sites we now have in play.

**There are so many different types of businesses out there, so why did you choose management rights?**
When I made the decision to leave a secure career in retailing, I looked at many different businesses. I had a background in news, but I had to ask myself if I wanted to work in a news agency as an owner/operator and accept that I would be there seven days a week, from five a.m. to seven p.m. And with no appreciable cooking skills, I never had a dream of owning a restaurant or fast food franchise.

The thing that excited me and led me on the management rights path was how I could make money and increase my business net worth.

**How do people select which type of management rights suits them?**
There were so many options to consider in this industry, such as holiday buildings, permanent letting, student accommodation, commercial rentals and business centres. But the overarching decision for me was how I could increase the turnover and the value of my business.

Many of my clients will make the choice that suits their family's needs. Often, young families may decide on the slower pace of a permanent letting complex. Many of them have larger homes or apartments and reduced office hours.

Several or my more mature-aged clients have opted for a smaller resort by the sea, which provides them a less hectic lifestyle due to fewer units and a wonderful location to relax and enjoy the restaurants and beach areas. Apartment sizes are generally smaller, but when it's just one couple, they don't need a big space.

**What are the next steps a new manager should take after acquiring a complex? What did you do?**
Everyone wants to improve their business and make more money. The second, third or fourth business you select may push you in a different direction. You may start off with a small permanent or holiday complex and move on to buy a much larger building. Or you might enjoy a change and decide to move to a busy holiday building or corporate opportunity if you feel the need to challenge yourself.

You could also decide to invest in another business from the equity you've created or even buy a second complex and run them at the same time.

My journey took me from a small holiday complex to owning two complexes within three years. My focus changed, and I formed Bluechip Resorts Pty Ltd., which led to supervising several properties at once during the next seven years.

Within ten years, we owned student accommodations, holiday buildings from Palm Cove to the Gold Coast and permanent buildings.

All of those options are available to you, which is unique to this industry. There are so many diverse types of businesses with different demand levels that are dependent upon your selection. You can be in control of your destiny and determine how busy or relaxed you would like to be. As your needs change throughout your life, you're able to fit the business to them.

**How did you find the right business?**
The golden rule I've always lived by is, "Surround yourself with people you can trust and are experts in their field".

I found it helpful to look at every option first. It gave me an appreciation of the different types of businesses available. Sometimes that journey can be a bit daunting. I reviewed properties in the Gold Coast region, as this was the area where I wanted to stay. It suited our family. The children were in local schools, and there were many different options available.

The internet wasn't as well-developed back then, but even now I suggest to clients that a personal inspection is critical. The location of the complex, the standard of the apartments and facilities and the general 'feel' of the business is important to assess, and you can't get that from looking at a website.

Being driven by opportunity and increasing income also played an important role in my journey. I surrounded myself with agents I could trust and felt were listening to what I told them we were looking for. I was guided heavily by their expert advice and fell in love with a holiday building by the sea. I had visions of running down to the surf every day for a late-afternoon swim.

The agent knew what I was looking for in regard to opportunity and income. He guided me to a building on Chevron Island that was only one year old and had been set up by an experienced operator. All units were in the letting pool, and the apartments were furnished identically. He knew this would be the right building for me to settle into and improve the value as it matured.

**Why do you believe people lose interest in their management rights?**
People lose their passion for the industry in many different ways. Some may have simply bought the wrong building for their level of experience or personal needs. Others find that after two or three years, they desire a greater challenge. As with every industry, there are constant trials to be faced.

My experience is that often those people who leave the industry early have been presented with an erroneous expectation of what the job is all about and have been sold into the wrong building. The reality is that you're buying a 'relationship rights' and not a 'management rights'. This is very much a people-focused business, and you must have the ability to understand the demands of servicing all the various stakeholders.

**What limits people's success in management rights?**
Again, there can be many limiting factors. These include the following:

- Fear of failure.
- Poor training.
- A lack of skills in relationship management.
- Being unaware that one of the greatest assets you sometimes need is a short memory. My motto is, "Let things go, and move on to the next challenge!"
- Neglecting to ensure they've surrounded themselves with experts who will help them navigate through the purchase process, which can have a long-lasting effect on their confidence.

### How did you get into corporate letting, and what did you learn from it?

After four years, I made the decision to take a break for six months and try my hand at other industries. I needed some excitement and missed interacting with people, so I entered an area of the industry I hadn't yet been a part of and became involved in a partnership purchase of a large corporate building in Brisbane.

One of the things that kept me in the industry was the great diversity of business types you can be part of and own. That's why I think the industry is so dynamic. You can be as busy or as passive as you desire, depending on what you buy and how you structure running the property.

### What challenges have you experienced, and how did you overcome them?

One of the greatest challenges is the adversity of Mother Nature. From cyclones to bad weather, holiday buildings can be dramatically affected by these events.

Having been through major cyclones such as Yasi in Northern Queensland, I understood that it's not only the preparation for the event, such as contacting guests to make them aware, but it's also about the aftermath. There's no electricity, and damage has been done to the common property and units. You're not only dealing with the internal repairs, but you're also reliant on tradespeople who will be flat out in the area handling other people's repairs.

With any type of adversity, you simply need to attack the trees before the forest. By identifying what can be done to get yourself operational, and then getting everything else handled based on their level of importance, you'll be able to work through a difficult situation. As with everything in our industry, the golden rule is, *Don't panic, stay calm, and develop a flight path.*

## Could you share your management rights formula that made a difference in your business?

In holiday buildings, there are many marketing avenues to consider. There's no silver bullet that allows you to magically be 100 percent full. I've always looked at all the options for getting 'bums in beds'.

The industry has evolved in this area. When I started, the travel agents were the predominant source of bookings for many buildings. Last-minute sites weren't yet established, and the internet wasn't as widely used for people booking their own travel.

I recognised early on that the secret of success for my holiday businesses was outstanding service and repeat-based clients. It's five times harder to get a new client than it is to retain an existing one. If people enjoy outstanding service from you and have a great experience, they will return again and again. Many people talk about how guests no longer have any loyalty to properties and just select the cheapest deal they can find on the internet. I disagree with this position.

## With so much accommodation information online, how do you compete?

While there are more choices than ever before, and travel has become far more accessible, people are creatures of habit. If the holiday was everything they wanted it to be, they will come back. We recently worked with a building in Yeppoon that opened as a holiday building. Within twelve months they were taking over 50 percent of its bookings from repeat-based guests. By delivering outstanding service, they established themselves quickly as the premier building in the area.

There are many examples of experienced operators at Coolangatta, Broadbeach, Mooloolaba and Noosa that have high occupancy rates due to their exemplary service. By putting the emphasis on keeping the customers happy and providing a great experience, you can set your holiday business apart from the competition.

**How long does it take for a management rights business to make money?**
Making money in your business depends on many factors. Some buildings with a proven track record will provide good returns after one month. New, off-the-plan buildings may take up to six months to establish a client base and get the revenues up. Those considering such projects may not receive the immediate revenue benefits, but the decision to purchase is also about the improved selling price they're likely to receive.

I've always looked at what the business could potentially be worth at sale time, as well as the cash flow it's likely to generate along the way.

**What are the best ways to market your management rights business to your owners, prospective tenants and guests?**
The marketing for holiday and permanent buildings is entirely different. Permanent letting is mainly generated through the internet and signage located at the property highlighting your vacancies. More managers are realising the advantage of marketing vacancies to their existing tenants, as many of their families and friends may enjoy the experience of visiting their friends.

Holiday buildings require a much broader brush. Short-term websites, wholesalers, telemarketing, voucher sellers and repeat-based customers all have to be nurtured. Once they're at the resort, it's up to you to make sure your building is first in their mind when booking their next holiday.

### What are the keys to success in management rights?
Understanding your relationship with all stakeholders, and being able to provide outstanding service, are very much the keys to success. The caretaking is just as important as the letting. If you provide outstanding service to the committee and the owners, the management experience becomes far more enjoyable. That attitude then becomes infectious with your staff and flows onto your guests and residents.

### How do you transition from a regular job to management rights?
If you want to transition from one to the other, my best advice is to try and fully understand the industry you're moving into and select the building that best suits your needs. There are some wonderful training and education courses provided for new entrants to the industry. Talk to as many people as you can, so you learn from their experiences.

### Have you had a management rights/business that failed?
When the Global Financial Crisis (GFC) hit in 2009, many businesses suffered not only a loss of income, but also a loss of values in the multiplier. We have a business on the Gold Coast that lost money due to the multiplier dropping.

There's always a risk; but when you consider the dynamics of most businesses you can own and operate, management rights is a highly secure investment. The multipliers are now higher than they've ever been because the banks have confidence due to the business model of providing better services to the body corporate, residents and guests in the buildings.

**Why do you think some managers falter within the first six months?**
I talk to managers all the time and explain the importance of looking at what they've purchased, and that they need to fully understand it before they start changing the world.

There may be obvious compliance issues or marketing improvements that can be made in the short term, but it's important to touch and feel it as a business.

**How do you keep up with social media and technology, while making sure your business is ahead of the game?**
People are now heavily influenced by social media, including sites such as Trip Advisor and booking.com. They review star ratings and comments, and get a general feel for what other travellers think of the property.

People now also use Facebook to pass on their thoughts regarding their travel experience.

As an operator, you can embrace the technology and encourage it as a positive form of marketing. Websites are now highly interactive and provide a great opportunity to constantly update and change your offer. Encourage those guests to post comments if you feel their experience has been a good one.

**What are some methods of growing a management rights business?**
There are five simple ways to do this:

1. Provide outstanding service to your guests, residents, body corporate and all stakeholders.

2. Understand your market, and develop a customer-based marketing plan.

3. Look at improving your offer constantly, such as upgrading apartments, complex facilities and common property.

4. Seek advice from industry experts regarding what has worked for them and what you can take back for your business.

5. Operate on the 90/10 rule. Don't get bogged down or concerned about the 10 percent that doesn't go right. Concentrate on the positive 90 percent.

**How do you motivate yourself to complete the tasks you're reluctant to do?**
Personally, I would always handle them first. I'd meet the challenge head on when I'm at my most willing. It's always a great feeling to overcome that activity and then focus on the items you do enjoy.

**Do you have a morning routine that sets the stage for your day?**
I'm an early riser, and though my routine as a consultant is much different compared to my resort management days, the principle is still the same. I would always plan out what I wanted to achieve for the week and review anything that would take significant time to plan or complete.

Our industry is dynamic, so I always allow myself some 'allocation time' to respond and react to the current situation.

As a resort/complex manager, many of the tasks you undertake are the same, but you're always challenged with different circumstances. Being able to respond and react to whatever you're confronted with, and do it with a smile on your face, is a winning formula.

**Do you have any funny stories you'd like to share?**
In management, there are many different situations you'll be confronted with as you begin your journey. There's one story that sticks in my mind from when I was managing a holiday complex on Chevron Island.

I received a phone call from an apartment in which the power had gone out, and the two women were scared to be there in the dark. I told them I was on the way and assured them all would be well.

Upon arriving at the apartment, I asked if they'd turned on any appliances recently before the power went off. They explained that they'd been heading for bed and couldn't remember if they had or not.

I checked the power box and could see that the main switch had been tripped.

I tried to turn on the circuit breaker, but it immediately tripped off. Then the women remembered that they'd just turned on the ceiling fan prior to going to bed.

Bingo! I knew that was it, as the direction switch has often been a problem with these old fans.

I asked one of the women to stay next to the power box, while the other assisted me by holding a torch. I placed a towel I'd brought with me over the bed and stood on it to reach the ceiling fan, as we couldn't fit a ladder into the room.

Once I'd identified the switch and turned it in the right direction, I asked the woman to turn the power on.

Success!!! But then I heard a slow growling noise, and I became concerned that we had a bigger problem

I asked the woman at the box to turn the power off, but still the noise continued.

How could this be?

Eventually, I was resigned to not being able to stop the noise, and we turned the power back on everywhere.

Once I climbed down from and removed the towel, we identified the issue. My two guests had positioned a selection of sex toys on the bed prior to the lights going off, and I'd accidentally started one of them.

They both turned bright red, but as any good resort manager will tell you, your response is always to enjoy a good laugh and move on.

## The seven wisdoms from this chapter:

1. Surround yourself with experts.

2. A personal inspection is critical to get a general 'feel' for the business. It's important to assess the management rights, and you can't get that from looking at a website.

3. To establish yourself in the industry, you'll need:
   - well-run systems and procedures
   - a great marketing strategy
   - excellent customer service
   - a clear reporting structure
   - a good presentation
   - a sense of routine.

4. You can be as busy or as passive as you desire, depending on what you buy and how you structure running the property.

5. You're buying a 'relationship rights' and not a 'management rights'.

6. Acquire a short-term memory. Let things go, and move on to the next challenge.

7. The golden rule is: *Don't panic, stay calm and develop a flight path.*

# FREE GIFT

Danny is offering readers of *The Management Rights Formula* a complete, tailor-made operations manual for your first building purchase.

This manual will
- improve your efficiency and save time
- ensure services are delivered consistently
- save you 60 percent in training costs when you recruit a new staff or relief manager.

Danny charges between $1,500 and $2,500 for this operational manual, and you can have it for FREE.

To access this awesome gift, please visit:
**www.mrformula.com.au/bonus**.

# CHAPTER THREE

# Jason Fu

## Show Me the Money: What You Need to Know to Succeed

*" The most important word in the world of money is cash flow. The second most important word is leverage."*
~**Robert Kiyosaki**

Jason Fu was born in mainland China and came to Australia at the age of eighteen as an overseas student. He worked hard to develop his English language skills and improve his academic knowledge, and completed high school with an Overall Position (OP).

Through the University of Queensland, Jason successfully attained his CPA qualification, became a full member of CPA Australia and was ranked number one in Queensland in the Taxation segment in 2009.

Jason completed his Master's Degree at the Queensland University of Technology, where he developed his expertise in international accounting, forensic accounting, business analysis and valuation.

Utilising all of the expertise he'd picked up along the way, Jason established his own business, Goldenwater Mortgage Services, in 2014.

Backed by his expertise in accounting and an inter-professional perspective, he and his team have been heavily involved in management letting rights and offer alternative options to all his clients, in order to set them on the path to achieving their goals.

Jason considers his family the most cherished part of his life and is grateful to have them by his side on his life journey.

## What made you want to start your own business?

People talk about success a lot more nowadays. But to achieve it, you need to have dreams and goals at the outset. Starting up your own business is definitely one way of making this happen.

I have no doubt some people inherently have a life purpose, and I admire them for it. However, like many of us, I'm not one of the fortunate ones, so starting my own business hadn't even crossed my mind.

But after years of being an employee, I decided to take the risk. I worked in big and small organisations, and resigning from my last regular job came so naturally, I've never looked back.

Do I consider my years working in organisations wasted? The answer is a resounding, "No!" The skills and expertise I developed throughout those years set me up for the challenges of starting my own business, and I appreciate every minute of it. I have no doubt there will be many more *aha* moments in the future that will make me realise the importance of the skills I learned from just one of my jobs.

I believe everyone has the intent to be of value to others in society; yet most don't know how to go about it. Back in the day, I thought being a model employee would fulfil that need for me, so I worked towards it. Then four years ago, I made a conscious decision to start my own business, so I could add value to our society and leave a legacy for future generations.

I'm sure my goals will evolve again and again as time goes on. However, I believe that whichever path you take, whether it's starting a business or being employed, if your purpose isn't clear, you should constantly work towards figuring out what it is by setting and achieving incremental goals. These small achievements along the way will most certainly contribute to attaining your most stunning greatness.

## What made you decide to service the management rights industry, and how are you contributing to it?

We're here to serve a purpose, which is to capitalise on our skills and resources. This enables us to secure our clients the necessary funds to start or expand their business portfolio and achieve their goals.

The management rights (MR) business utilises this particular model, which is a perfect gateway for people who wish to transit from being a typical employee to a business owner. At the time of this writing, the regulatory environment for MR is well established in Queensland, Australia. And as an industry, its volume continues to soar quite rapidly, due to the growth in population and demand for new residential and commercial property developments. Meanwhile, this market is at its infancy stage in other states, including NSW and VIC, which could translate to continuing future growth in the industry as a whole.

Back in 2015, when we decided to have MR lending as our strategic focus, we realised the policies were written with unbelievable concentration by a small number of lenders and their business bankers. Although it seemed an easy decision for clients in terms of who to choose for their MR lending needs, we considered it a major risk. The magnitude of the aftermath regarding these particular lenders making major policy changes would be unimaginable. But considering the way new businesses were written, these changes were almost inevitable.

We saw it as an opportunity, as well as a duty, for us to step in and offer alternate options.

Since then, not only have we proposed insights and second opinions to existing operators, we've become the first point of contact for numerous business brokers, industry solicitors, accountants and other stakeholders, when they need MR lending information and solutions. We also started our own Management Letting Rights workshop series, where we invite experienced industry professionals to join forces and offer all-round solutions to new and existing operators.

During the time I've been directly involved in the MR industry, I've developed an immense passion for it and become an absolute advocate. This is exactly the reason why I'm sharing my insights and journey here. I'm hoping to help new industry entrants to not only make a living, but also prosper in this business and grow the industry even further.

**How can someone become successful in the management rights industry?**
I think it's paramount to get a few basics right, so before you enter into management rights, you need to ask yourself these questions:

1. What is my purpose for entering the market?

2. What strategies should I pursue to ensure my goal is achieved?

3. What is my exit strategy?

At the very fundamental level, are you in it for the lifestyle or the business development? Are you easing into retirement or building up a business venture? You're not right or wrong in pursuing either, yet your purpose dictates the types of strategies you should adopt, which I divide broadly into two strategies: offensive and defensive.

- **Offensive strategies**

    These comprise strategies that enhance your value proposition as a caretaker and on-site manager. Offensive strategies should include:
    - Improving service quality regarding caretaker duties and promoting your value as an on-site manager.
    - Undertaking activities in which you're constantly seeking to gain additional letting opportunities.
    - Becoming a solution provider, rather than order taker.
    - Investing in both short- and long-term marketing strategies (conventional and digital) to raise brand and service awareness.
    - Asking for referrals and following up on prospects.
    - Reinforcing a rapport already in place with the owners, body corporate managers, tenants and all other stakeholders.
    - Becoming an activist for the industry and taking initiatives to promote it.

    All of these strategies aim to improve the letting component of the business, while maintaining a solid performance with caretaking duties, both of which are key to the appreciation of the business value.

- **Defensive strategies**

    Defensive strategies involve focusing on maintaining the status quo of the existing business, without aggressive growth plans and actions. These strategies may include the following:
    - Carrying out your duties to a satisfactory standard, as specified in the caretaking agreement.
    - Advancing systems to improve efficiency and reducing costs.
    - Maintaining the current letting pool and cultivating harmony within the complex, such as hosting events.
    - Implementing processes for preventing, detecting and mending issues with both caretaking and letting duties.

## Is having an exit strategy also important?

Regardless of how much you love the business or how long you've had it, you need to think ahead and develop an exit plan. Here are three common strategies, all of which, if done successfully, can deliver great value to you as the business owner.

1. **Selling**

   Have you created a sustainable business, so a successor can easily continue delivering value to owners and tenants?

   If so, the market may be willing to pay a premium for it.

2. **Investing**

   Have you developed a robust system to the point your staff can operate the business, and you can pull back from the daily operations, or even become a passive investor of your own business?

   If so, it will continue to create value, which you may invest in even more businesses.

3. **Educating**

   Have you accumulated sufficient knowledge, expertise and resources that you can capitalise on it by providing mentoring, coaching and training services, so more people can benefit from your experience?

   If so, you might be able to embark on a whole new adventure.

At the end of the day, these purposes, or strategies, are by no means mutually exclusive. I believe most operators will have a mixture of all of them and may even swing back and forth from time to time. Ultimately, your vision guides your actions.

**What are some of the challenges in management rights, and how can they be overcome?**
I'm a strong believer that management letting rights (MLR) is a 'people' business that comes with all the bells and whistles of interpersonal dealings and interactions. In fact, from the moment you embark on the journey of purchasing an MLR business to the day you sell it off, you have no choice but to deal with the vendor, selling agent, property owners, committee members, body corporate manager, tenants and suppliers. And typically, the interactions are carried out on a personal level in an ongoing basis. How you maintain a solid relationship with all these stakeholders is the key to making your daily life as an MLR operator more joyful.

One example we see quite frequently is how crucial it is to develop and maintain a trusting relationship with the vendor in order to have an MLR business run smoothly and become successful.

People often see a buying/selling transaction as a zero-sum game, as the benefits seem mutually exclusive between the vendor and purchaser. This is why many first-time buyers negotiate so fiercely on the purchase price, to a degree where the relationship between the buyer and vendor is beyond repair at a preliminary stage.

What they fail to realise is that a business transaction like this often involves a prolonged process, with a range of factors that can make or break the deal. And oftentimes, the issues that arise during the process require experienced management rights sales specialists to work with both the vendor and purchaser to resolve them. Some typical issues include the following:

- Insufficient access to the vendor's system and documents that are needed for carrying out the due diligence process.
- Requiring extensions for financial verification, legal due diligence and finance approval.
- Having a better offer presented to the vendor during the purchasing process.

For a complete list of issues that may arise, please go to **www.mrformula.com.au/is**, where you can find an experienced management rights sales specialist who can play a key role in resolving them.

**What are some of the challenges of MLR from a financial perspective?**
As a mortgage broker, I find that MLR operators often neglect certain regulatory and finance requirements. These are some examples:

1. **Not acting on the term options when needed.**
   This results in shortened agreement terms. Of course, you can rewrite an agreement, but it's better to always keep the term as long as possible.

2. **Not maintaining satisfactory performance.**
   This results in breaching finance agreements with the lender.

3. **Not having the appropriate paperwork on file relating to caretaking and letting duties.**
   This creates confusion in the future.

These issues could easily be resolved if you remain vigilant, review all the requirements regularly and engage responsible industry professionals who monitor and remind clients about their requirements and due dates. Go to **www.mrformula.com.au/reminder** to get a list of key dates for management rights agreements, and never miss one again.

## What crucial decisions have had a profound impact on your business?

Since the mortgage broking industry in Australia came into existence in the 1980s, it's evolved quite substantially. Now, thirty-odd years later, the industry has an established presence in the market, introducing more than 50 percent of all residential mortgages to lending institutions nationally.

Along with a strong industry presence is the ever-intensifying competition within the industry itself. We experienced this firsthand as one of three companies embarking on different mortgage businesses around the same time, about four years ago. Three years later, one of the owners had become a banker, while the other had moved on to the construction industry. We were the only ones to survive.

Porter's generic strategies are comprised of cost leadership, differentiation and focus. One year into our operation, we made the decision to change our strategic focus and offer business and commercial lending, in addition to our ongoing residential lending commitment. Later on, we narrowed that focus even further and set out to become the MLR business lending specialist in the market, echoing Porter's cost leadership/differentiation/focus strategy.

When we conducted a business analysis, we made the following discoveries:

- MLR business lending is complex and specialised. Purchasers may not always be able to find a reliable source for assistance and are not able to collect accurate and timely information. It always lacked broker intervention, so clients are often blindfolded throughout the process.
- Because we're qualified accountants, we maintain the habit of scrutinising information from all parties, which is crucial in gathering and presenting information required for loan approval.
- Instead of providing all-round services to satisfy all markets, we perceived that concentrating our entire focus and resources on satisfying the needs of a smaller segment was the best way for us to add value to the market and make a real difference.

The decision to change our focus wasn't taken lightly, yet the transition was effortless. The MLR market appreciates the value and options we offer, which is why our strategy has caused us to experience exponential growth and now constitutes 85 percent of our overall business lending.

## How can people in management rights stay motivated and inspired on a daily basis?

We live in a world that spoils us with instant gratification.

From product designs and retail promotions, to personal goal setting, everything and everyone keeps saying that you can have whatever you desire instantly, and the products or services that satisfy this need are rewarded with your attention and resources.

Unfortunately, at best this overdose of instant gratification may not always be motivating, and at worst it can even de-motivate you, simply because it implies you can expect rewards with limited or no effort. When you then realise that isn't the case, you give up quite easily and feel disappointed, before moving on to pursuing other goals, which may again fail to give you that instant satisfaction. This is because true and enduring happiness doesn't come without sacrifice and hardship, so the cycle goes on, leaving you more and more depressed.

Staying motivated, in my opinion, takes a long-term vision, coupled with *passion, discipline and practice*. It's also about recognising that constantly pushing, hustling, failing and then rising up again, usually over a long period of time, is where success comes from and is the key to providing ultimate satisfaction.

True passion can go such a long way. This burning desire inside you means you're willing to sacrifice all other resources to make it happen. Think about the effort the top athletes in the world put into becoming great.

At the same time, I would argue that not everyone knows exactly what their own passion or life purpose is when they're young, so they often choose the easier path of not even trying to find it.

This is why you need discipline, as I unequivocally believe passion is fundamentally developed and internalised throughout the course of your life. While you might envy the young people who discover their passion early on, put in the hard work and achieve great results, I believe it also works the other way around. What I mean is that putting hard work into whatever you're doing, giving it your blood, sweat and tears and becoming great at it, may just help you discover your passion.

Then, of course, you need to practice being motivated and inspired. Having the skill of trade and the willingness to put in the hard work for its own sake, can drain you quickly. Surround yourself with mentors and peers you can talk to, those who've 'been there, done that'. These are the people who will tell you, no matter how excruciating the journey may be, that it will all be worth it in the end, and you'll see a brand-new landscape. Get to know what they've been through and how they faced and broke through the obstacles. Learn how they stayed motivated, and then implement these actions into your own business and life. Call it faith. Brainwash yourself into believing you're motivated. Tell it to yourself over and over again, and it will happen!

Find or develop a passion. Strive to become the best, and don't settle for anything short of an amazing achievement.

## What do you believe holds most people back from achieving the financial success they desire?

Consistency and change.

At a glance, you may believe these two words have opposite meanings, so please allow me to explain.

People view freedom as being able to do whatever they want. However, if your desire is to hurt another against their will, there's a problem, as the other person doesn't have 'freedom' from you doing harm to them. I'm not trying to get philosophical here, but let's just say, in a free society, people enjoy their freedom within certain rules and boundaries.

The same logic applies in regard to your goals.

I believe there are two fundamental elements that hold people back:

1. Inconsistent goals
2. An inability to adapt to change

These two ideas are often more intertwined than you may realise.

- **Inconsistent Goals**
  
  Many people fall victim to the desire to satisfy themselves instantly, so they discount the value of future success.

  This means that when you're confronted with two choices, whichever one is perceived to bring you immediate value is usually your pick, despite the other option possibly generating more value over the long run. Nevertheless, not long after you made the choice, you soon realised that it won't come to fruition, so you jump ship and start on something else.

  There are a lot of success stories, especially over the last couple of decades in the technology realm, that seem to have happened overnight. Thanks to the internet, this impression gets amplified when more and more people tell their stories as if they occur all the time. Not surprisingly, success begins to appear within easy reach, and achieving it any other way becomes unacceptable.

  What the general public fails to realise is that numerous heartbreaking failures take place prior to this 'overnight' success that are left untold. These success stories only became reality because they kept their long-term vision consistent, stayed in the fight and remained resilient. Despite all the obstructions along the way, they pushed through and came out the other side.

  In my opinion, maintaining a consistent vision, and always rising up after falling down, is exactly the kind of consistency that's required to deliver success.

- **Inability to Adapt and Change**

  With the constant pressure from the market, such as customers, suppliers, the government, financiers, and everyone in between, businesses face uncertainties all the time. The ability to change in a prompt and swift manner and adapt to the new market conditions is becoming more and more crucial for anyone who wants to survive and flourish.

  From my old accounting days, I learned this important cycle for implementing change in business, which I still follow:

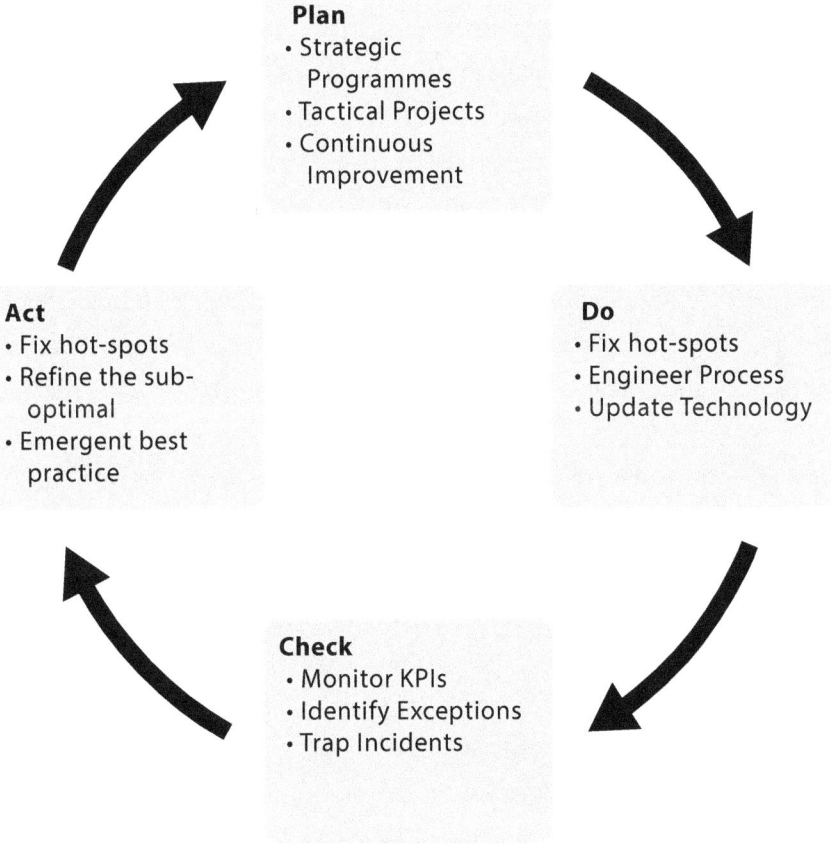

Figure 1: Source: https://improvedapps.com/wp-content/uploads/2014/02/Change-Cycle.png

In this day and age, as suggested in the book *The Lean Startup* by Eric Ries, the time used to complete the cycle and fine-tune the process may be a luxury you no longer have. He proposes that regardless of the size of the business, everyone is facing the same time and resource restrictions, and you need to constantly implement changes with a rather unpolished, raw product or process and seek instant feedback for improving it. He calls this 'minimum viable product'. It means that if you're not connecting with your potential customers by pushing out your product in a timely manner, someone else is going to, and you will lose your customers for good.

Although this seems to suggest, in a broad sense, that consistency is applicable at a strategic level, while change impacts the tactical and operational planning and execution, this is not always the case. The pursuit of consistency and the ability to change are more intertwined than ever. There may be situations where you have to change your vision, because it's become outdated for unperceivable reasons, from maybe ten years ago when it was originally set. While consistency is required before you can determine whether an implemented change is producing results, you need to find the right balance between consistency and change for yourself and have the capability to pursue both.

### How do you motivate yourself to complete a task you're reluctant to do?

A few years ago, a participant in a reality show claimed that she treated failure as an opportunity to experience something she wouldn't have been involved in by choice.

Her response resonated with me.

You have more than enough choices every day, in almost every aspect of your life. For example, you can choose a new career, form new relationships or even select a restaurant. Now, more so than ever, you have the power to choose what you want to do. As a result, you're missing out on a lot of options and experiences you might not have considered.

Essentially, you don't want to do something, because you're unable to anticipate the sufficient value of that undertaking, or you perceive that by making a more familiar choice, the value will then be secured. It's risky to do something you're not comfortable with.

So, then I'd like to ask, "How did the options you feel comfortable with become comfortable in the first place?" Didn't you have to experience them for the first time without knowing how they were going to turn out?

A better question may be, "If you always have comfortable options available, and the power to choose them, when do you get to have new experiences that will deepen and broaden your life?

My rule for myself is that whenever I'm faced with a choice of whether to undertake a new task, I always default to saying yes, unless there are good and logical reasons not to, and I certainly hope this practice will enrich my life with all the fulfilment I couldn't have anticipated.

## How do you stay organised?

I've heard about studies claiming disorganised people may be more innovative and efficient than their organised counterparts. Despite their reasoning and findings, I personally feel that a methodical approach works best for me. Don't get me wrong; my desk gets cluttered over time, which somehow fits in with my work routine. Yet a medium-to-long-term vision always deserves a well-structured action plan.

I'm results-oriented and firmly believe that being organised starts with precisely defined goals. If a goal is merely something that would be nice to have, the plan can be in a less structured format. For instance, write it on a Post-it note and stick it to the computer monitor.

On the other hand, if the goal is a must, I would always first write it down or draw a picture of it. Then by doing the same for my current position, and laying it out side-by-side with my well-defined goal, my action plan starts to emerge.

I always find the S.M.A.R.T. model works wonders. It specifies that the goal should be:

- **S**pecific
- **M**easurable
- **A**chievable
- **R**elevant
- **T**imely

The details of each term can be easily found all over the internet, yet one habit I did have to get myself used to was being true to myself. The goal-setting process is extremely personal, despite it being used for business teams. This particular model works best with short-to-medium-term goals, which I call 'tactical goals'. Once the main goal is set, it should be regularly refreshed and updated as these smaller goals are achieved, because the aim is to make your ultimate life purpose more vague, until you get closer to it and are able to be more specific.

Overall, while you work towards your life purpose far ahead into the future, you need to have a goal setting and action system that incorporates methods such as the S.M.A.R.T. model, and implement it with devotion. For example, depending on the size of your goal, you have a number of options:

- When aiming for a medium-term strategic goal such as expanding your business, break the actions down into monthly or quarterly targets.
- If you're going for a short-term operational goal, such as meeting sales targets, do weekly or monthly action plans.
- For daily tasks, have a to-do list, fine-tune the process, and develop a habit of completing the tasks in the most efficient manner possible.

Regularly review these goals and action plans, and make improvements as needed.

Once the system is in place, strictly follow it, and take out the human emotion and discretion whenever possible. You'll discover that tasks will get done in a far more organised fashion.

**How does someone choose a loan structure, and what should they look out for?**
This is where I get technical.

Similar to many other aspects of life, your brain is hardwired to make decisions based on factors that are clear-cut and concrete. In a typical purchasing transaction, negotiating interest rates and fees is probably the top priority for most newcomers, and even some experienced operators. It's only second to negotiating on the purchase price. However, you do have much more at stake than these factors.

I would like to propose a couple of scenarios here, both of which are real-life cases:

1. Assume there are two lenders that will consider the deal: one has a slightly better interest rate and fees, while the other lends more. Which one should you go for?

2. Assume two lenders are offering identical products with the same fee structure: one has a better appetite for approving the deal, while the other has friendlier subsequent conditions. Which one is a better option?

This is where you'd generally break the finance components down and tackle the real issues behind each situation, as every circumstance is different. What I do is broadly analyse the following aspects of a particular transaction:

- **Lender Appetite**
  This considers whether a particular lender is likely to approve a loan for a certain MLR purchase or refinance. Factors may include the following:
    - The size and location of the business.
    - The type of business, such as holiday versus permanent letting, motel or student accommodation.
    - The level of experience the purchaser possesses in the MLR and related industries.
    - The exposure this lender already has for the location/type/borrower experience.

- **Borrowing Capacity and Loan-to-Value Ratio (LVR)**
  These are determined by the existing and proposed income, as well as your current financial position. Here are the elements you need to consider:

- The borrowing capacity the total income is able to service (such being able to repay the loan when due).
- The level of expenses to maintain your current lifestyle.
- The existing financial commitments of the business and its key associates, which includes directors, shareholders and beneficiaries, as well as their spouses and dependent family members.
- Other real and non-real assets in your possession, and the equity that's readily available.
- Whether there's sufficient funding to cover:
  - the amount required to complete the transaction, including the deposit, government charges, finance costs and other incidental costs
  - the shortfall due to lower valuation and/or reduced loan amount as a result of additional risks as assessed by the lender.

- **Loan Structure and Terms**

For purchasing an MLR business under the accommodation module, your income will need to be able to service the loan over fifteen years or the remaining term of the letting and caretaking agreements, whichever is shorter. For standard modules, the maximum agreement term is ten years, so the maximum loan term matches the remaining agreement term.

Once the loan term is determined, and servicing is demonstrated, you have to look at the actual structure, which includes asking the following questions:

- Who was the purchasing entity for the business and the unit?
- How was the purchasing entity structured by the accountant?
- Are there additional securities offered as collateral?

- Is there an equity release from refinancing existing loan facilities?
- Should you combine all the borrowing into one business loan facility or keep the loan for the manager's unit separate from the business loan?
- What does it mean to have a three-year loan term with renewal requirements, as opposed to a fifteen-year business loan with a thirty-year facility for a residential loan?
- What annual review requirements are applicable to the lender/facilities?

- **Product Features**

This section relates specifically to the bells and whistles of the loan facilities themselves, and each feature has its implications. Here's a simple table depicting the pros and cons of Interest only (IO) and Principal and Interest (P&O) loans:

|    | Pros | Cons |
|----|------|------|
| IO | Lower monthly repayment required, thus less pressure on cashflow. Savings can be set aside, which means they're readily available for use. Has the flexibility to further lower your monthly repayments by making extra repayments. | Doesn't reduce loan balance. Fluctuates automatically based on additional repayments made, as well as interest rate changes. May mean higher risks, especially when losing letting units and value of the business. The borrowing capacity may be reduced, as remaining principal and interest (P&I) period is shorter. |

|  | **Pros** | **Cons** |
|---|---|---|
| **P&I** | Accumulates 'forced savings' from required principal repayment. Extra repayments reduce interest component from each P&I repayment, thus shortening the loan term. Reducing the loan balance also reduces the risk from operation fluctuations, such as lost letting units/business value. For residential loan facilities, it could mean lower interest rates in today's market. | Cashflow pressure due to required principal repayment. Principal repayments made are not accessible without a formal request and approval. Repayment amount remains the same, even when extra repayments are made. |

- **Fixed versus Variable Rates**

    Despite these two interest rate types seeming equal and mutually exclusive, the fact is that interest rates are, by nature, variable, and constantly changing. They can be artificially 'fixed', which is only temporary. This is why the fixed rates are generally for a short period of time (one to five years) and are modified quite regularly as well. A quick note is that most lenders offer a rate-lock option for a certain period of time for a fee, which secures the quoted fixed rate, yet you always have the option to void it if the rate drops at settlement.

    Most fixed-rate products don't allow unlimited extra repayments. You'll generally incur a break cost if the loan facility is closed during the fixed period, and it can be substantial. This is where you need to take the long-term approach and plan for any potential changes in the business, in order to minimise costs.

- **Redraw or Offset**

  There's an easy way to understand the difference between these two features:
  1. Redraw is a function of the loan facility itself.
  2. Offset is a feature of a separate savings account when linked to a loan facility.

  But you need to take caution, as despite their similarity in terms of reducing interest expenses, there may be very different methods of operation with each lender, as well as significant tax implications, for operating the accounts. You'll need to speak to your accountant if you have any concerns.

- **Other considerations:**
  - **Equity versus income**

    There's a common confusion in regard to the borrowing capacity of equity and income. To put it simply, they work independently when the borrowing amount is determined, and the lender will then take the lesser of the two when deciding how much to lend.

    For example, John has a three-million-dollar property. It's unencumbered, he's willing to offer it as security and assumes the lender is willing to loan 70 percent against this property. So by his calculations, he can borrow $2.1 million based on his equity.

However, the profit from the business John is buying may only support a loan amount of $1.5 million. So assuming there are no other issues, and all approval conditions are met, this is the highest amount the lender will approve.

- **Timing**

    Another important aspect for a loan application is timing. Generally, the lender will commence an MLR loan application assessment only after all critical documents are in place. This includes the financial verification and legal due diligence report, which typically take fourteen and twenty-one days respectively, from the contract date to complete.

    Once the reports are ready, and all other critical documents are collected, it takes another fourteen to twenty-one days for the complete assessment of the application, during which time a valuation of the manager unit and/or the business is completed, and any additional enquiries get addressed.

    How long this all takes should also reflect the time of year and the lender's workload, which goes hand-in-hand in most cases. For example, it may take much longer to assess a finance application around the holiday season than other times of the year.

I should note these factors strictly relate to the offers and requirements of conventional lending institutions, like traditional banks. There may be other types, such as private lenders, who are willing to make a loan based solely on security, regardless of whether sufficient income can be illustrated.

However, they're generally short-term solutions that need to be restructured over to the conventional lending institutions for it to make economic sense for the long term.

Similar to many other aspects of the MLR business, finance can be a lengthy topic on its own, and this is exactly where your experienced mortgage broker can add value to your business, so you can keep growing.

## The seven wisdoms from this chapter

1. Regardless of how much you love your MR business, or how long you've had it, you need to think ahead and develop an exit strategy.

2. Management rights is a perfect gateway for people who wish to transit from being a typical employee to a business owner.

3. Use an experienced and knowledgeable management rights sales specialist who understands how to develop and maintain a good relationship with the stakeholders during the contracting process.

4. To stay motivated and inspired, you need to surround yourself with mentors and peers who've demonstrated success in what you want to achieve.

5. Be consistent with your goals but also be willing to adapt.

6. When choosing the right loan structure, you need to break down the finance components and tackle the real issues behind each situation, as every circumstance is different.

7. In the MLR business, you need an experienced mortgage broker who can add value to your business, so you can keep growing.

# FREE GIFT

Jason is offering readers of *The Management Rights Formula* a free complete, tailor-made VIP financial review consultation, valued at $550.00.

This will save you significant time, as he'll only present management rights within your price range and will help you set up the correct loan structure for tax savings and expanding your portfolio.

To claim this amazing gift, visit **www.mrformula.com.au/bonus**.

# CHAPTER FOUR
# Michael Joseph O'Farrell

## Break Through Your First Million, Systemise, Build a Team and Increase Your Profit

*" Great things in business are never done by one person. "*
~Steve Jobs

Michael is the executive chairman of the Australian Holiday Resorts (AHR) Group of Companies, as well as the chairman of Australian Offshore Investments (AOI) Group of Companies, which was established in 2007. AOI holds property interests in Brisbane and the Gold Coast, as well as investment and management links in the UAE.

In addition, Michael has served as the president of Lakelands Golf Club, GC, has been a member of the Australian Institute of Directors and served as a board member on various sporting and body corporate committees.

In 2005, he purchased the Riverside Hotel and lifted the occupancy from 62 to 82 percent, increased the yield from $69 night to $133 night and the number of room nights sold to 30,000.

## What services and accommodations does the Riverside South Bank Hotel provide?

At South Bank Riverside Hotel, we like to think of ourselves as a smaller boutique, almost family-style building. We've traditionally been referred to as a mum-and-dad operation, however we also cater to the semi-corporate and quasi-government crowd. We're close to the cultural centre of Brisbane, so people from all over will come here to see the shows. When someone checks in to the Riverside, we try to make them feel welcome and provide them with a five-star experience.

## How many years have you been in the industry?

Well, when we started on the Gold Coast, we were in a busy building and handled everything from school groups and football teams, to everyday families. We lived there for nine years, and even though we've been at our current property since 2015, we still get people asking us when we're coming back to the Gold Coast, but those days are long gone.

## From your experience, what would you say is the most important issue someone should know about before entering into the world of management rights?

Management rights is an interesting business, because there are so many stakeholders that have an obvious interest in what you're doing, all the way from a guest or tenant, the owner and the body corporate, to your own family and business.

In management rights, as in any business, you have to deal with all different kinds of personalities. People will push their own agenda at the expense of others, so what I learned is that you must go back to the one constant: the building. This means everyone needs to connect by working towards what's best for it. If the building looks good and is going well, then everybody associated with it will be happy.

## What advice would you give to someone looking to purchase a strata hotel to manage?

Well, the Riverside is a hotel, but it's also strata titled (individually owned), so I have experience in this area. What I can tell you is that it's a little bit different from, say, buying a Sheraton or Marriott. Generally, if you're buying a management rights hotel, you're going to virtually be a boutique-type business. You have a number of hotel studios, where the maximum size is a one-bedroom style unit, so you're going to have studios that will be twenty-five to thirty square meters, with a bed that's fifty-five square meters, and then you have to market to people who prefer this type of unit.

On the other hand, if you're buying an apartment-style complex, you're open to a lot more opportunity. You can have anything from a one-bedroom to multiple bedrooms, or you can have combinations.

So if you're getting into hotel-style buildings, you need to be accurate and proper in what you're marketing, because you're going against the Marriotts and Sheratons, as well as other big chains. This means you need to set yourself up accordingly. Never ever oversell yourself, but look at what other services you can provide to give the guest more bang for their buck. For instance, you might offer free parking and include wi-fi and breakfast.

## What specific strategies are required to keep your owners and committee happy and continuing to support you over the years and with different buildings?

As I said, the most important aspect of management rights is keeping everyone happy. For owners, they're pleased if they're getting a return, so you have to be able to produce rent that gives them a good return on their investment. That's what it's all about in the end. People don't buy something just because they like you. They want a return.

**How do you get a return on your investment?**
Do right by your guests, while also making sure they come downstairs and spend that extra dollar. The only way you do that is by building the relationship right from the beginning, so it becomes a cradle-to the-grave situation.

Now if all of that's working, and you're current in today's market, then everybody's happy and in the same boat, going in to the right direction. But it all starts with giving the owner a return on their investment.

**What's your secret for selecting the people to be on your team, and how have they worked together so well?**
Well look at me. I'm smiling all the time. Maybe too much, because sometimes a smile tends to give you away. I was supposed to be a cranky old man who's been in this business forever.

I don't operate it hands-on anymore. I've surrounded myself with good middle management who are young and fit. And because I've given them enough autonomy, they feel there's kind of ownership of it.

The one big point you need to instil in anybody who works for you is that they're on a team that all wants the same thing. It doesn't matter if you're the general manager or the cleaner. Once your staff understands that, then you're going to have a successful business.

We like to think that our environment allows for a bit of levity, but they need to be serious when it comes down to doing business. I'll get lots of people saying it's always a pleasure to come here, because they're treated well. I won't stand for anyone having a bad attitude.

**Do you have a top tip for inspiring them to perform at their best?**
I think I might have mentioned this earlier, but it's about communication. You need to put a lot of time and effort into setting up your team and giving them clean guidelines.

From the start, you let them know what their duties are, their level of autonomy and authority and how and when they should report to you. But then you can't come in six months under the stewardship and move the goal. It will make them believe it's impossible to reach.

And when you put people in charge, you can't be nit-picky. You need to have respect for the fact that you picked them, so if they're not performing, go and look in the mirror. If your manager isn't performing, you have to give yourself a swift uppercut. Ask yourself if you're not talking to them enough. Or maybe the product they have to sell isn't there. You need to get to the bottom of it.

My general manager is fantastic. We're mates. He gives suggestions as to what to do and what not to do.

How did we get to that stage? I know his wife, and she's on my side. So if he gets lazy and tired, she'll kick him in the butt and tell him to do his job!

Everyone likes to be told they're doing a good job and to receive recognition. But sometimes they also need to hear what's not working, which actually brings me to a great point. If you see a problem in a certain area, and you tell them about it, you have to let them talk. If you keep talking, you've lost.

You can burn through staff if you come in tired and grouchy and never let them know they're doing a good job. So I have a rule. If I'm feeling or I'm off the boil, I stay away as much as I can. You need to give yourself time to calm down. And when you walk back in there, you're going to have a great attitude.

If you want to have words with your general manager, you never ever do it in front of everyone. Always approach it like you're going over to have a quiet chat. Then you make sure they have the tools to fix it.

In this business, you have to develop patience and give your staff the opportunity to recognise their own mistakes and turn it around, but do set a time limit and go back and check in with them to see if it's been corrected.

> *You don't build a business, you build people, and then people build the business.*
> ~Zig Ziglar

**Do you have any advice or strategies that have helped you remain competitive?**
Absolutely. It starts with the body corporate, right through to ourselves. You have to be doing something all the time. It's no good to be satisfied that you refurbished four years ago, so you're not going to bother with it. You have to build that bank all the time. But the trick is getting the

owner to agree. To do that you have to talk to them constantly. Keep reminding them of how wonderful it is that you're giving this return and that the body corporate levies remain at an acceptable point.

But you also need to be aware that in eighteen months to two years' time, certain changes need to be made. At this point you should ask them if they want to start contributing, and you'll hold that money in trust, or maybe they're already able to provide for the refurbishment.

The point is that you shouldn't ever make the refurbishment massive bill. You do little bits all the time. What I believe is that management rights is the art of becoming a valuable advisor to improve the return for the owners.

In regard to getting repeat guests, it's like if you're running a golf club, for example, and you want people to keep returning to a particular event. Never give all the benefits away at that first event but just enough to keep them coming back to receive even more in the future.

Some owners don't understand the role of an on-site manager who provides expert advice and services that add value to the building and owners. For instance, they know when and what to do to improve the presentation of the unit, which can increase the return on the owner's investment. An on-site manager may not clean and cut grass, which are both part of the caretaking duties. But they do perform a lot of other valuable services that owners may not see, so it's difficult for them to understand and appreciate this unique set of skills.

I've learned a lot from being in business over the years, and I always suggest taking the long-term attitude, so you can make sure your rate is in line with the competition.

### Whose role is it to communicate to the owners?

Originally, I was the one to talk to the owners. Well… actually… that's not a hundred percent correct. Originally *my wife* handled all communication with the owners and established a great relationship with them. All I had to do then was make sure we got the return.

But as the years went by, and we get bigger, we started doing things differently. I came up with an acronym years ago, P.B.O., which means poor bloody owner. Too many people in this industry forget that it revolves around the owner and not you, the body corporate, the chairman or the body corporate manager.

Yes, you might own a substantial business within the building, but you must respect the owners. Everybody has to be able to talk to them. When it comes down to the nitty-gritty, we have an owner liaison. Cradle to the grave again. If an owner has an issue or isn't happy with what we're doing, they just want to sit and talk or sell their property, or they want to get a permanent instead of a short-term tenant, we want them talking to us.

### What does a typical workday look like for you?

If you're a day-to-day manager, a typical workday can be the best or worst of your life. If you have the business acumen and drive to get into this industry, you understand the need to prioritise. There are times I have a full to-do list and then realise at the end of the day I haven't been able to do anything on it.

I know some managers who won't stop until they finish everything on their list, while others will leave it until the next day. The only problem is that the next day could be just as busy. It's difficult at times to prioritise when you have so much to do. You may have the plumber coming and the pest control people running around the building, when all of a sudden, the lift breaks down. So now you're on the phone to people to repair the lift. And it can happen. You might have a tremendous day's work planned, and the washing machine breaks or the toilets blow up. You never know what's going to happen, so you or your team members have to be ready to take care of everything as it occurs.

You're the manager, so you need to stay strong and project that you have everything under control.

We have standard procedure instructions (SPI), which is an old acronym from my corporate days for almost every event that can happen, from how to greet the guests to someone passing away.

**How do you relax and enjoy yourself?**
In the old days, if you received a letter, you could sit on it for a few days before writing your reply, and there was a week's turnaround. But with modern technology, people expect immediate gratification, so it's not easy to find time to relax.

For me, it could mean immersing myself in a hobby, going to lunch, playing golf or just going for a walk to clear my head. It could even mean talking with other people within different industries and appreciating that I have a good, stable income.

And it's not just the managers. It's the brokers, the bankers and the lawyers, as well. Just make sure you have someone you can ring up and ask what they're doing, and go do an activity you love.

It's important to have someone to talk to and bounce ideas off. You need someone who will back you up and give you support, even when you don't ask for it.

**What's the most important piece of advice anyone has ever given you?**
I'd say definitely from my mother. Due to ending up in an orphanage, I didn't know my mom until I was about eight or nine, and my dad until I was about ten, when we had a little bit of closure.

My mother had absolutely no education, but she went to the University of Life, and some of the things she told me were amazing. She always said, "Mike, if you can't be a cricketer, at least look like you're dressed accordingly. Put your lights on, go out there and say, 'Well I'm not playing for Australia, but I'm going to do the best I can.'"

The other great bit of advice she gave me was that you have to be all things to all people. Whether you're having sausages with the workers or caviar with the coin. I was the school captain. I've always been a leader and a boss, but I've never forgotten where I came from. We had to pass down our clothing, and we didn't get our first TV until I was seventeen. Even though I'm older and, relatively successful, I always try to remain humble.

We must never forget that we're all from different backgrounds. Some people have tried and failed where others have succeeded and become successful, but you must treat everyone with respect.

**How has staying humble helped you build a better team?**
I believe it comes from within. I've watched high-ranking CEOs and other executives within my industry be absolutely ignorant and arrogant and use their power to get away with not treating people with respect.

I understand that if you walk into a group of people, you need to let them know you're the boss, but you can still do it in a humble way that doesn't involve crawling on your hands and knees.

We have people who clean, and maybe that's what they'll do for the rest of their lives. But I can absolutely guarantee you those people are just as important as the general manager. You don't have to tell people all day, every day that you're the greatest. You do it by respecting and appreciating the job they do and taking an interest in their lives.

That's all people want. To be thanked and recognised for what they're doing and that you're genuine about it.

### What keeps you motivated and focused?
Grandkids! If I'm ever off the rails, which does happen, I look at my grandkids and always remind myself that they're the reason I put myself through compliance.

I do love it. Don't get me wrong. Sure, I'd be happier playing golf. However, the one thing that drives me is family. This is good and bad, because I have to keep reminding myself not to give them everything.

### Do you continue to practice your personal development?
Not a day goes by that I'm not learning something or trying to learn something. I'm not a particularly good student at English, but I'm developing my writing ability. Attitude is important. It's not that I sit there every night, but I'm always trying to develop my knowledge. That's why I believe strongly in continuing professional development (CPD). I'm even a member of the Real Estate Institute of Queensland (REIQ). I religiously do my CPD, merely because it's important to learn something new. I also sit on other boards and give advice to the newbies.

I read everything. I understand the agenda. I have the knowledge and comprehend what's going to be discussed at the board.

### What do you believe are the essential qualities of being a success?

You have to be honest and ask yourself, *Who am I? Do I want to leave some sort of legacy? Do I want people to say I was hard and tough, but I knew my business and did the right thing by the people who worked for me?*

If you're in business, then you have to be upfront. Yes, you want to make a quid, no doubt about that. But you also have to leave a little bit of meat on the bone for everyone else as well. If everybody's making reasonable returns, then you're being reasonable. But if you're ripping and tearing and gouging every cent out of people, or you're out to scam everyone, then in my opinion, you should not be in business.

### What do you think stops people from being successful in this industry?

Not doing their homework before they get into it. For instance, some people think success is about putting your feet up on the desk, smoking cigars and drinking tequila. If you don't understand what's involved, then you need to seek information about it.

You have to be prepared to work, and you need to be honest. We all just put our toes in the water until we know what we're doing. You have to move heaven and earth to make sure you know you're successful. Otherwise, why even make an attempt in the first place?

So how did I become successful? I worked at it.

### What's a big error people make once they become successful?

It depends where you are in your business and life.

The biggest problem I've seen is that lots of people who've become successful in one particular industry think they can take that success, or at least a part of it, to another one. I know I can't go and be a successful developer. It's not in my blood. Every time I pop my head into another industry, I get it chopped off.

**What are some of the main characteristics of your target customers?**
It never ceases to amaze me where customers come from and why they approach you. And of course, once you get a customer, how do you keep them? That's probably more important than getting them in the first place.

For instance, we'll have a group from Norway attending a conference, and we might only get one crack at them. So you may wonder why we should put any effort into making them happy. But they could go online and leave a negative review. They might not tell you, but they'll tell twenty or thirty others not to go to your place, because they received bad service. You have to make sure every customer, no matter who they are, goes away happy. I don't subscribe to the saying that the customer's always right, but I do subscribe to giving every customer the royal treatment, no matter who they are.

We get all sorts of people, from kids coming down for a concert, to families, to corporates. We treat everyone the same. Your customers come from everywhere. How you treat them is important.

Never judge a customer based on your first impression. Most of the time, you'll be wrong.

**What happens when you have to turn away a customer?**
There comes a time when you may not necessarily want a customer back. Now, you don't stand at the front desk, grab the keys and take them out. But unfortunately, you may need to let someone know they've been cancelled due to their attitude. It's a delicate exercise. Sometimes you just agree to disagree. We tell them we're sorry, and we do try to look after all these people. Yes, you

still might get a bad review from that person, but it's better to sever ties with someone, and they go away as reasonably as happy as can be.

### How has Airbnb affected your business?
Airbnb is an incredible concept that unfortunately is here to stay. And it's going to impact hugely on the industry. I always say if you're a building manager, you're in this industry. It doesn't matter if you have an owner that's in your letting pool, not in your letting pool or is a resident. If you're doing the right thing by your building, you're not going to have a major problem with Airbnb.

If you're not giving your owners a return, or if you're not close enough to your owners, that opens the door for them.

But it's not only Airbnb. It's outside agents, as well. If they're running around your business, then you're not in control of your building.

### How do you maintain control?
Through communication. You get it by talking to the owner. You never know when you're going to walk into a body corporate meeting and need an owner's vote, so you have to earn it!

You accomplish this by doing right by the owners. You have to be that person at reception they'll talk to rather than go to outside people.

### What are your top sales channels, and how important is it to still have face-to-face meetings?
We do around 30,000 nights a year here. Ninety percent of that, or 23,000 nights, comes from the internet. We then look at the three main producers of that 27,000: booking.com, Expedia and our own booking button.

So immediately you begin to understand that your relationship with online travel agencies (OTAs) is extremely important, and you get to them through booking platforms. But there are so many of them now. The one we use in particular is Site One, which distributes our inventory out to the hosts of thousands of OTAs.

The biggest barrier we've now maximised is our own booking button. We're always about trying to get our product at the top of the search criteria, so people will come to us directly, rather than through the other sources. And then hopefully when we get those people, we can do enough for them to keep them coming back. The other thing you need to do is allocate personnel, which means applying money towards it.

We don't do an enormous amount of face-to-face work with big organisations that have conferences here. We actually call on those people. We go and see them to make sure that when they're thinking of their next conference, or they have someone coming to town, that we at least get first crack. If we acquire that group, it gives us leverage, so we always make sure we put enough work and effort into it.

Regardless of the internet, you still can't beat the good old face-to-face process. I remember back in the nineties, when I first got into management rights, people would begin looking for a place months in advance of their trip and would book accommodations six months out.

Then you'd call every quote you'd given out that week and ask each person if they'd made a decision. If they hadn't, but they gave you the date they'd be making up their mind, you made sure you let them know you'd be calling them back on that day. Then you'd ring them, because if you didn't, someone else would, and you'd miss the booking.

But these days, we can be sitting at 40 percent in at nine a.m., and by ten pm that night, I could be booked out because of the internet and last-minute sales. That's life these days. People are so much busier, and you don't just do business in your little area.

## What is your top marketing strategy?

Generally speaking, if you're in a short-term business, such as holiday or corporate, and you have a large inventory of rooms, you want to be on the internet.

You have access through major OTAs, but the most important thing you need to make sure of is that you get your own website ranking as high as you can.

You have to invest the money in advertising, so that it's written the right way with the correct content that includes certain keywords and the accurate language Google will recognise, so take the time and spend the money to get it done.

Now if you're in a smaller business with less inventory, where you rely more on static advertising fees, you'll be talking to people on the phone or in person, which means you need to have selling ability. Too many people might be successful in the business world, but they don't have the right background to know what to say to get that order.

How many deals are you going to get if you never ask for it? Zero. If you're face to face with a prospective client, what you're doing from the moment you sit down is asking for the order. You close it!

If you're a mum and dad operation, you're in a smaller building, and you're relying on short or even long-term guests, it doesn't matter. The same principles apply. You have to do the work, because that's where you get your enquiry. Make it as easy as possible for people to come in and do that inspection. Welcome them, and sell the building and the service.

## The seven wisdoms from this chapter:

1. Everyone needs to work together to do what's best for the building. If the building looks good and is going well, everyone associated with it will be happy.

2. Understand your targeted customers and how to market your products to them.

3. Continue to improve the building to stay competitive.

4. Manage the cash flow to ensure money is always there for repairs, so your building stays in top condition.

5. Consistent, meaningful communication is vital. Respect is mandatory.

6. Have a break to recharge, so you can perform better.

7. When face to face with a prospective client, from the moment you sit down you're asking for the order. You need to close it.

# FREE GIFT

Mike O'Farrell and *The Management Rights Formula* team are offering readers a free webinar on the step-by-step guide to attracting and retaining talent.

If you're a manager who want to have a million-dollar business, please go to **www.mrformula.com.au/bonus** to join the webinar.

# CHAPTER FIVE

# Sylvia Johnston

## Turbo Charge Your Profit: Make Your Technology Work for You

*" Our business is about technology, yes. But it's also about operations and customer relationships."*
**~Michael Dell**

Sylvia Johnston is co-owner of HiRUM Software Solutions, which recently celebrated their twenty-year anniversary. During this time, they've seen a lot of changes and have enjoyed being part of the evolution.

Having begun their careers working in the accommodation industry, the people at HiRUM know firsthand the daily opportunities and concerns of property managers and hotel operators, and have made it their mission to provide technological solutions that will enable their businesses to run more efficiently.

To date, they've achieved many milestones, including being the first company worldwide to offer an online booking platform that allows guests to book directly with their clients.

HiRUM's channel manager was created to ensure that clients have a choice of solutions within the Australian market, while simultaneously maintaining cost efficiencies. Their latest mobile-first technology provides seamless mobility across all departments, an accomplishment as yet unseen within the industry.

HiRUM is privileged and humbled that their solutions have been so influential within the accommodation industry, and that they've significantly improved the lives of their clients.

HiRUM helps managers run a successful business and live the lifestyle they desire.

## What made you choose this path?
My husband and co-director, Phillip Johnston, and I have worked in the accommodation industry for most of our lives, first in England and then in Australia.

In 1997, we stumbled upon a basic piece of technology that required some TLC. We believed that with focus and determination, we could one day evolve it into a powerful technology stack that would streamline hotel operations.

We began by developing the tools we always wished we'd had access to when we were running our own hotels. Back then, a lot of our ideas seemed more like science-fiction and fantasy, but fast forward twenty years, and we've far surpassed even our own goals and expectations.

With firsthand experience in running hotels, we feel we have a great understanding and insight into what our clients need. This is what has allowed us to develop such powerful and highly sought-after solutions.

## What does HiRUM do?
Simply put, we develop technology that helps property managers improve their business and increase their profitability, while also providing them with the means to enjoy the lifestyle they long for.

The dream of a relaxed way of life is usually one of the main reasons people go into management rights. However, upon buying them, many newcomers find they're restricted to their desk. HiRUM changes the game by providing them with the mobility to run their business on their own terms, across all departments, from anywhere.

**Who do you help and what do you provide for them?**
We help all kinds of businesses and business owners within the accommodation industry, such as hoteliers, property managers and management rights operators, as well as marinas, caravan parks, B&Bs and student accommodation. The list is endless. No business is too big or too small for HiRUM products.

We provide clients with a seamless end-to-end solution, thus increasing their profitability by selling their inventory for the best price, across the world's most effective channels and providing cost-saving efficiencies to their businesses.

Because we free up our clients' time, they can focus on important tasks such as guest service, product delivery and other valuable activities. We've always invested our profits back into the solutions we deliver, ensuring our clients have the state-of-the-art tools they require, which negates the need for a myriad of different solutions. This saves our clients both time and money, not just in the products they use, but in labour efficiencies throughout their businesses.

**How has working in the industry helped you in assisting others?**
Having been employed in all sectors of the industry, we, as the owners of HiRUM, know the challenges operators face. We've been there. We've encountered the same hurdles and frustrations. We know that seamless, integrated technology is the key to taking the pain out of everyday operations. We believe it's our duty to give back to the industry that has given us so much.

**What is the greatest service you provide for your clients?**
We provide the perfect end-to-end software solutions for all aspects of accommodation and management rights. This saves our clients both time

and money, not just in the products they use, but in labour efficiencies throughout their business.

## What is your mission?
Our mission is to make our clients' lives easier and less stressful; also provide them the profitability and freedom of lifestyle they desire.

Our motto is that there's no success and there's no failure. There are only outcomes, which are a product of the things we imagine, the risks we take and the path we choose. If the outcome isn't what we desired, we simply re-evaluate our path and try again. But we must never lose our imagination or become averse to the risks it forces upon us.

## What does a property manager need to consider when purchasing a property management system?
The first thing to consider is which is preferable: an on-site solution, a pure cloud solution or a combination of the two.

HiRUM's whole development plan, first and foremost, is focused around the need to continue with a premise-based solution. We believe if the underlying platform can cater for any scenario, your business will never be interrupted.

Ideally, the solution you choose should have the ability to run either on-site or be accessed via an external server. This allows a full range of options for the property manager, along with some great risk management solutions overall.

A property shouldn't rely solely on the cloud, as dependency on the internet should be mitigated at all times. A pure cloud solution generally becomes worthless when the internet falls over. While some areas within Australia have incredible internet, others have almost none. Couple this issue with the unpredictable weather that frequents our shores, and the recipe for disaster increases.

**Is it more beneficial to rent or buy your software outright?**
HiRUM has long recognised the need to provide the industry with the option to buy their solution outright. As such, we provide perpetual license options to all our clients. We now appear to be the only company offering this option for property management software (PMS), which is disappointing to see.

By not offering a perpetual license, companies lock users into staying with a solution that may no longer suit their business needs. But the risk of losing access to their historical business data is so scary to consider, they remain stuck with it.

As the average lifetime of management rights ownership falls within the two-to-four-year timeframe, the most affordable short-term option for managers is usually to rent their solution. This generally eliminates large monetary outlays for something they may only require for a relatively short period of time.

Renting also often includes ongoing software maintenance and upgrades as part of the overall annual fee. This affords the manager the opportunity to budget accurately. However, the option of purchasing outright should not be dismissed as renting does come with a drawback: data within the software is held in a database, and without the relevant program in place to open it, the data itself can't be accessed. For example, you can create a letter in Microsoft Word, but if the program is later removed from your PC, then you'd have no ability to open the document you originally created.

Where business data is involved, it's generally imperative that ongoing access to this information be made available, and therefore an option to purchase the solution is needed. An outright purchase could be financed through a broker and spread over the envisaged length of ownership, resulting in similar monthly payments to any rental agreement. This is definitely an important consideration when choosing a provider.

**What kind of support is available?**
Support, and its subsequent pricing, varies between systems. From online self-help tutorials, videos and work sheets, to person-to-person engagement via phone or internet, there really are many options available across most products.

However, there's something more important to consider, which is the level of onboarding and training offered by the new provider. An onboarding process that personally takes a customer through the product and thoroughly trains them, will reduce any frustrations down the track.

It doesn't matter how many times you've been through the purchase process, there are always challenges when taking on a new property.

At HiRUM, we believe it's important to take clients through the process step by step, in order to ensure the journey after the property purchase is as smooth as possible. Doing so gives them peace of mind in their investment. This is the reason we developed our HiRUM Onboarding Program that provides our clients with a dedicated team member to ensure their management rights journey starts correctly and is set up for success.

## How well does the software cater to trust accounting?

Managing trust accounting for owners is a serious business with strict compliance mandated by the government. Therefore, it's important to use a provider that has a robust solution incorporated into the software and not just an add-on module, as many in the industry offer.

HiRUM is renowned in the property management industry for our trust accounting capabilities. Not only does our software provide precision accounting and transparent record keeping, but our accounting wizards ensure lightning-fast speed. This enables property managers to focus on other important matters like delivering great guest experiences.

## Does the property management software (PMS) integrate with third parties to provide a full solution?

Integrating with third parties always comes with risks. Having two or more products communicating effortlessly together at all times requires each supplier to be respectful of one another. If one provider makes a change to their product that impacts the seamless communication of the other without giving sufficient warning, the client can be left in limbo as they scramble to make the two ends knit together again.

Channel management, online travel agents (OTAs) and PMS products are classic examples. These three providers have to work even harder in this arena, as technology is forever evolving.

The risk for problematic integration is reduced when several of the connectivity pieces are provided by one supplier, so all of them are designed to work seamlessly together. This ensures the best outcome for the customer.

HiRUM is one of only a few companies in the industry worldwide that can provide a PMS and channel manager designed and built to work together as a single, integrated end-to-end solution.

## What do property managers need to consider when thinking of changing systems?

If you're changing systems due to perceived reduced cost, then second thought should be given here. Many systems may seem cheaper on the surface, but when you look at the hidden costs, such as the rate per user and mobile device, most systems on the market are quite comparatively priced.

## How important is sufficient training?

To ensure a new system is ready to go, staff needs to be fully trained. This cost (time and money) can be considerable, depending on what system you're moving to. This point cannot be underestimated, but often property managers are led to believe it will simply happen at the flick of a switch, which isn't the case.

## How open are your owners to change?

Database structures differ considerably, and there's no easy way to export and import between solutions, contrary to some companies' claims. The owners need to consider that the look and feel of the data output will differ. But they often dislike change, and receiving a foreign-looking income statement without any warning could be unsettling for them.

This means you need to always ensure every point of contact within your business is aware that change is coming, so they can plan accordingly.

## What is a channel manager, and what needs to be considered when selecting one?

A channel manager enables you to sell your inventory via online distribution channels. It feeds your real-time availability and rates up to the relevant channels and then sends booking details back to your PMS.

These online channels are responsible for the majority of bookings for most properties, so it's increasingly important to make the most of consumer buying habits and maximise your potential bookings by connecting automatically to these high-traffic online sites.

## Can your system connect to all major online booking channels to provide access to customers worldwide, and do these channels include the complete connectivity hierarchy?

You need to consider your property. Where do most of your clients hail from? Your channel manager should provide you with the best opportunities to connect you with your target market.

Our system, HiSITE, is the leading Australian channel manager, connecting properties to all the major online booking channels from the complete connectivity hierarchy, including:

- online travel agents (OTAs), such as Wotif.com, Booking.com, Expedia, Agoda, C-Trip, HomeAway and Airbnb, amongst others
- metasearch channels, such as Google Hotel Ads, TripAdvisor and HotelsCombined
- global distribution systems (GDS), such as Sabre and GTA.

### Does the channel manager integrate with relevant partners?

The system you choose needs to integrate with your property management system (PMS), central reservation system (CRS) and accounting programs such as MYOB, Reckon and Attaché.

It also needs to allow for your property's availability to automatically upload in real time from your PMS/CRS to all booking channels and vice versa, as well as permit reservations from all channels to feed directly into your PMS. All of these save you valuable time and expense.

Most people don't realise that many channel managers are, in fact, third-party providers to a property's PMS provider. This increases the opportunity for something to go wrong. The more moving parts of the machine, the more opportunity there is for one section to break.

Choosing a PMS provider with an inbuilt channel manager ensures that the products were made to work as one, so syncing issues are dramatically reduced. This is a major bonus for the property manager who relies heavily on the success of the channel manager and PMS working together.

HiRUM is proud to be in the unique position of providing our clients with a complete end-to end-solution, where the PMS and channel manager are purpose-built to work together with no need to worry about third-party add-ons.

### Is the channel manager user-friendly?

It's important to have a user-friendly system with a live dashboard that's easy to understand. You need to be able to view the information and updates from each online booking in one central place, and the system should be easy to navigate and provide detailed reporting that makes budgeting and forecasting a stress-free process.

HiRUM believes in transparency and accountability. With the HiSITE Channel Manager, property managers know their position at a glance. They can see a live overview of their property's active channels, rooms and connections, which enables them to easily identify any issues before they have a chance to interrupt the property's performance.

## How effective is the system in managing inventory and controlling pricing?

Property managers often tell us that they prefer to automate the process of managing inventory 24/7. This is where HiRUM's channel manager comes to the rescue.

Once you set your preferences and a threshold is triggered, HiSITE IP will automatically adjust your rates based on availability and update your inventory and booking channels. Then it will close out channels based on your preferences to ensure your rooms are always listed at the best price.

## What marketing tools are included?

Marketing is made simple if you have access to online promotional tools that allow easy and comprehensive setup of promotional campaigns, competitive offers and pricing codes.

HiRUM's promotional tools help create urgency, increase awareness and drive bookings. From special promotional codes to stay pay offers, we have you covered.

**Does the system offer a range of analytics to help people predict future trends and grow their business?**
Property managers need to quickly and easily see which channels are delivering the most bookings and which are not.

With HiRUM's inbuilt reports, you can better manage your business, sell your inventory and predict future trends.

**How long will your new system take to implement, what training is provided, and how much help does a person receive after the initial purchase?**
In today's fast-paced world, you should be looking for a company that provides a good mix of assistance, including fast emergency technical support and online resources like tutorials and videos.

As a property manager, your business and personal life will be transformed when you choose a channel management system that provides these advanced technology features.

HiRUM offers a comprehensive number of support options that will ensure you have help whenever you need it.

**To cloud or not to cloud? That is the question!**
Many software vendors tout the cloud as being 'the be-all and end-all' for doing business. At HiRUM, we believe the cloud is set to be pushed aside, making way for the next generation in technology, which is 'mobile first'.

When the cloud became a reality a few years back, many managers breathed a sigh of relief. They believed their information was safe and sound in a cushion of floating security, as they were no longer restricted in accessing what they needed when they needed it. They wouldn't lose data or private information if their hard drive crashed or have to transport that information everywhere they went. Suddenly, managers and business owners had the capability of logging into the cloud and accessing their information no matter where they were.

But as time goes on, the cracks have begun to appear.

Too many property managers across the globe have been subject to cybersecurity concerns, along with performance issues due to poor internet connectivity. This has left them searching for a solution that offers greater security, and at the same time freeing themselves from worry over a poor internet connection.

They now have discovered that what they need isn't pure cloud solution, but something that can be used from anywhere, anytime, without internet dependency.

We at HiRUM fully understand these concerns. A dedicated team of software engineers is working to develop a solution that arms managers with the right tools to effectively operate their business from anywhere at any time, without being reliant on the internet and solves those important security and internet concerns, while providing the opportunity to work flexibly.

We feel the future for property managers looks brighter than ever with greater security and flexibility available to those willing to embrace innovative technologies.

## How can property managers increase direct bookings and reduce their reliance on OTAs?

Most Property Managers have a love-hate relationship with online booking/travel agents (OTAs). They appreciate the bookings that come through them. However, they often gripe about the large commissions and that they don't 'own' the customer booking.

Given this circumstance, property managers are constantly searching for ways to increase their direct bookings. Here are some ideas:

- **Use your data to increase direct bookings and customer satisfaction.**
  Personal customer service has always been vital to the travel and accommodation industry.

  With the increase in data being collected from guests, hotels should be able to personalise their marketing and communications to meet modern consumer expectations. This not only makes for a better experience, but is proven to increase retention and conversion.

  According to research from *Accenture*, people are 65 percent more likely to buy from a business if a promotion is relevant and personalised. Hotel guests want—and expect— accommodation providers to use the information they've already supplied for unique offers and highly tailored messages.

  Your PMS holds the key to unlocking a wealth of data about your guests and their needs, thus encouraging new and repeat direct bookings.

- **Understand that 'one-size-fits-all' marketing communication no longer cuts it.**
  Everyone appreciates the personal touch, and this applies to the marketing received online. The same research from Accenture shows that 65 percent of consumers say they would be more likely to spend money with companies that remembered their purchase history, 56 percent on companies who recognise them by name and 58 percent if they recommend options based on past purchases.

  Businesses that try to appeal to everyone might end up satisfying no one. Be clear on your target market by analysing your past guests. Look at their state and postcode to determine the areas they travel from most. Keep records of your guests' characteristics to determine if your perfect customers are families, businesses, youths, retirees or another prominent demographic. Everything you do to promote your property needs to be done with your perfect guest in mind.

- **Continually gather guest intelligence.**
  Email addresses are essential for communicating with your guests online. Staff should be trained to capture the contact details of anyone who enquires, so you can build a list of guests and prospects. When sending email campaigns, be sure to address your recipients by name, remind them how long it's been since their last visit and mention their home state to impress your guests and keep them coming back.

- **Know that your PMS data is your goldmine.**
  Your PMS should be recording as much information as it can relating to your guests, such as addresses, preferences/likes, activities, spending habits, special anniversaries/events and birthdays. Utilising

this data in creative ways can help you create customer loyalty, repeat business and increase the lifetime value of your guests.

Here are some ways you can utilise the data to build guest loyalty and generate return bookings:

1. **Develop location-based promotions.**
   Filtering data based on state and postcode gives you the ability to send highly targeted communications to your past guests. For example, you could invite those within a two-hour driving radius to return for a weekend getaway, with a discount or add-on incentive if they book direct.

   Alternatively, if guests need to travel a longer distance to your destination, notify them when a discount airfare becomes available for their city.

2. **Send promotions based on annual events.**
   If you have a major annual event that occurs in your area such as a music festival or sporting competition, you can notify past guests to prompt a return visit.

   Those who've stayed at your property at the time of the last event may appreciate a reminder or opportunity to re-book early for the next one.

3. **Reward Loyalty.**
   Reward your loyal guests by offering exclusive deals based on their booking history. Make a point of contacting them

when they've had multiple stays or spent a certain amount at your property, to encourage another visit. Ensure these thresholds are realistically attainable, and offer rewards that are high-value. This can serve as an informal loyalty program to encourage repeat business.

4. **Remember special events in your guests' lives.**
Use the information you've gathered about your guests to send an invitation, exclusive offer or gift to redeem at your property in honour of their special day/event.

This same strategy can be applied to business travellers like sending them lunch menus. Also make note of scheduled events, such as their quarterly meetings and award dinners, and offer special deals.

- **Make guests feel valued through communication.**
In the lead-up to a guest's stay, encourage them to book local tours and activities through your services. Welcome them on the day they check in, and remind them of any important information about their stay, such as arrival procedure and wireless internet details.

Shortly after all guest departures, send a thank-you note. This process is great for building rapport and encouraging repeat visits. Upon checkout, guests should also be invited to provide a review that can be promoted on your own website, or to rate their experience on third-party review sites. These reviews will help future guests make the decision to stay at your property when seeking accommodation in your area.

- **Don't forget your previous guests.**
  Keeping in regular contact with guests will help you maintain your relationship with them.

  Remind them you're still there. Let them know about promotions, seasonal offers and any other newsworthy information they may find relevant based on the data you have about them. By keeping your property top of mind, your guests are more likely to return for another stay and/or refer you to friends and colleagues.

  If hotels and accommodation providers want to excel at marketing, they need to focus on personalisation. With the increase in data that's being collected from customers, hotels should be able to personalise each guest's communication and service.

  There's an overload of content, products and services out there. By providing a personalised experience, particularly one that's proactive rather than reactive, properties have a real opportunity to deliver much-needed value in an increasingly noisy world of choices.

  By using HiRUM's PMS, property managers can easily keep track of guests, their location, stay details, special events and spending habits. Using these powerful tools, they will be able to develop and execute professional marketing campaigns to convert previous guests and enquiries into new bookings.

- **Use Google to your advantage.**
  Consumers are often time poor and can be frustrated by how long it takes them to simply book a room on the internet. They no longer

want to search dozens of sites online to find different pricing for the same room wherever they go.

Likewise, properties are frustrated by the ever-increasing cost of generating new business, along with how little engagement they now have with what they see as *their* client prior to arrival.

Metasearch solves this by allowing the traveller to compare costs against hotel direct pricing, all in one easy location, so they can book directly with the property. Using this medium, hotels gain the advantage of a distribution network that isn't an online travel agent.

Metasearch is a service offering an extension of a property's own direct booking engine. The marketing is provided free of charge, with payment only required when a result (booking) is made. We call this cost per acquisition or CPA.

Use Google and other meta channels to bring bookings to you without the high costs of traditional OTAs.

HiRUM has teamed with the three leading metasearch brands that meet our strict criteria, thus bringing benefit to our clients. All of these providers present the opportunity of offering direct-to-property business at a lower cost than traditional OTAs, thus allowing the property manager to own the client relationship from the outset, while saving money.

- **Optimise your website to increase direct bookings.**
  Many people don't realise their website is their most influential marketing tool.

When people book online, even through an OTA, it's most often the property's website they visit for information on the facilities, to view photos and read past guest reviews.

Given this new consumer reality, it's imperative that a property's website is optimised to convert these visitors into paying guests and increase direct bookings.

- **Make it easy to book at your property.**
  Your booking mechanism should be simple, visible, and most importantly, able to drop directly into your PMS, to ensure no over-bookings are made and revenue opportunities are optimised.

  Using our two-way, real-time online booking engine, HiSITE Direct, removes the need for allocations and manual loading of availability and pricing. It's designed to work on any device, whether it's a phone, tablet or computer.

- **Throw away your enquiry forms.**
  Most people expect to book whenever they choose, so making them enquire first will significantly reduce conversions. Some website providers build in enquiry forms by default, so make sure you ask why this is being done. Not only does it result in fewer direct bookings, but they may be syphoning *your* data!

  Linking directly to your booking form will allow your potential guests to view your availability, rates and promotions all in one place, enabling them to book there and then.

- **Don't send your guests packing.**
  It's important to keep your guests on your website. Linking to external sites may send them on a journey of no return, making it possible for them to get caught up in a new search and forget to come back. Or they may get distracted by another property that pops up.

- **Ensure your site is mobile-friendly.**
  Responsive websites adjust the layout using fluid templates, which ensures your website is optimised for viewing on all devices such as desktop and any form of mobile or tablet, and ensures the best user experience.

  Also, the more mobile-friendly your site is the more favoured it seems to be in Google search results.

- **Promote your reviews.**
  Guest reviews help people make a decision when searching for accommodation. According to TrustYou, 95 percent of visitors read guest feedback prior to making a booking decision. After price, it's the most important variable people consider when booking a hotel.

  Given this fact, the importance of including positive testimonials on your website can't be overstated.

- **Keep up with technology.**
  There's nothing worse for a visitor than going to a website where the information is outdated, whether it's pictures of the property, invalid specials, old testimonials or incorrect contact information. To ensure your website is up to date, you should undertake a web assessment at

least every twelve months, in addition to keeping your information current on a monthly or quarterly basis.

- **Keep page load times to a minimum.**
Don't bore your potential customers. People don't like to wait for web pages to load. Most have an approximate one-second tolerance. Websites with a faster page load will often rank higher in internet search results.

- **Create engagement on your site.**
Customers love to interact with websites that have active content and provide the latest specials, competitions and relevant information about activities, both at your venue or in surrounding areas.

  Links to your property's social media profiles may also help generate engagement.

  Whatever you do, the aim is to keep customers engaged on your site. The longer you keep them there, the more likely they are to make a booking.

## What should property managers look for or avoid when choosing a website design company?

- **Choose a provider that understands the accommodation industry.**
The accommodation industry is complex when it comes to bookings, so it's important you choose a website provider that understands the industry and knows how to convert visitors into paying guests.

  One of the most important considerations when sourcing a website provider is to make sure they can integrate your booking form with your PMS and channel manager, to ensure your stock is always kept current. This eliminates over-bookings and optimises your revenue opportunities.

- **Make sure the provider uses an open-source platform, so you can make changes to your website whenever you choose.**
  It's critical to ensure your website provider uses an open-source platform. This allows you to edit content with ease, without needing complex website building skills or having to rely on a third party to make changes.

  Using an open-source platform also means that should you need to change website providers at some point, you're not locked into a proprietary platform; the website is truly yours.

  HiRUM uses WordPress, one of the world's leading open-source platforms to build our sites. This ensures our clients can easily update information without the need to pay for changes.

- **Use a provider that will allow you to own your website outright.**
  Some providers offer to supply you with a relatively cheap or free website in exchange for a percentage of booking revenue. This may at first seem attractive; however, what many accommodation providers don't realise is that it's much cheaper to pay an upfront fee rather than shelling out a commission model (percent of bookings) where you're locked into an ongoing cost beyond a reasonable payback period.

  HiRUM websites work on a minimal upfront fee, with *no* ongoing commissions, thus ensuring our customers own their websites outright.

- **Don't use travel agents to produce your website.**
  If you decide to use a travel agent to produce your website, be mindful as to how they capture data. Travel agents tend to host the booking form on their servers, which enables them to siphon the contact data, if they're so inclined, to use in their own marketing activities. One way to check this is to click on your booking form and other pages where data is captured and see where the url links to. If they don't link to your site, the travel agent may be hosting this data and can hold the details of all people who've either contacted you or booked with you.

As outlined previously, a property's website is critical to the number of direct bookings they receive. Whilst there are many pitfalls to avoid, if you do your research, and are fully aware of potential downfalls, there's no reason why you can't build an effective website for your property with minimum cost.

HiRUM builds conversion-optimised websites that ensures just three clicks from look to book.

> *We wish you much success along your management rights journey!*
> **~The Team at HiRUM Software Solutions**

## The seven wisdoms from this chapter:

1. The right technology can free your time, so you can focus on important tasks such as guest service, product delivery and other valuable activities.

2. Use state-of-the-art tools for running your businesses to save time and money.

3. Whatever solution you choose should have the ability to run either on-site or be accessed via an external server, in order to allow a full range of options for you and your staff, along with some great risk management solutions overall.

4. Choose an onboarding program that provides you with a dedicated team member, so you can ensure your management rights journey starts correctly and is set up for success.

5. Don't change systems just based on price. When you look at the hidden costs, such as the rate per user and mobile device, most systems on the market are comparatively priced.

6. Your channel manager should connect you with your target market.

7. With the increase in data being collected from guests, hotels should be able to personalise their marketing and communications, which not only makes for a better experience, but is proven to increase retention and conversion.

# FREE GIFT

**Sylvia** is offering readers of *The Management Rights Formula* a free website assessment for those who want to get more direct bookings, increase their occupancy rate and receive a website improvement formula.

To claim your awesome gift, visit **www.mrformula.com.au/bonus**.

# CHAPTER SIX
# John Mahoney

## Prevent Forest Fires: Strategic Legal Advice from Business-Minded Lawyers

*" Communication must be H.O.T., meaning, honest, open, and two-way. "*
**~Dan Oswald**

John Mahoney is one of the founding partners of Mahoneys and is widely regarded as the pre-eminent specialist management rights lawyer in Australia.

Since leaving his previous company and establishing Mahoneys in 2002, the firm has grown steadily. They now have the largest management rights legal team in Australia with more than ten lawyers working in the management rights area, covering the full spectrum of services, from buying and selling and dispute resolution, to advice, negotiating variations and extensions.

John has been intimately involved in management rights, as well as related legislation development and amendments, for almost twenty-five years. He is the author of many articles on management rights and lectured on body corporate law at the University of Queensland. He is also a past senior vice president of the Urban Development Institute of Australia.

John and his team are sought after for their experience in dispute resolution and negotiating outcomes without the need for expensive litigation. He acts for a number of diverse clients who own large management rights businesses, as well as one of the state's largest land developers and public companies.

Mahoneys is held in high regard by the industry at large for their expertise and how well they take care of their clients.

## What do you feel are the benefits of getting into the management rights industry?

Having been involved in management rights for over twenty-five years, I've been a part of many wonderful success stories. By and large, most people who buy management rights enjoy the business and experience of good financial returns and benefits.

The industry is well understood by many of the banks operating in Australia, and the comparatively large fraction of the purchase price they're willing to lend to buyers is an indication that they perceive it a relatively low-risk business.

## Why is management rights such a successful business model?

The reasons why the industry has gone from strength to strength, particularly in Queensland, includes the following:

- Management rights are well regulated by comprehensive legislation, developed and refined over many years.
- A large proportion of the income is derived from the caretaking remuneration, which is effectively a guaranteed source of income if the manager performs the specified duties.
- Because the two sources of income are easily traced, you'll have no problem ascertaining past financial performance. You're able to see the letting income through the trust account, and the caretaking income through the body corporate's records.
- Regarding contracts, the management rights agreements are largely where the value lies in such businesses, not intangible goodwill.
- The businesses suit people from all walks of life.
- For most management rights businesses, values are easily ascertainable, and there's generally a strong market.

While there are many legal technicalities associated with management rights, suffice to say that if you're contemplating buying them, and like most buyers propose to invest your life savings into the business, you owe it to yourself to use one of the few genuinely experienced management rights lawyers specialising in this area of law. At Mahoneys, we spend a lot of time sorting out all the issues that could have been avoided had they not used a cheaper alternative and come to us in the first place.

But instead of focusing on legal technicalities I will instead tell you about what a prudent buyer must watch out for when buying management rights and give you some tips on dealing with disputes should they arise.

- **Good work ain't cheap, and cheap work ain't good.**
  As with any businesses, you need to make sure you're not one of the small number of management rights buyers who doesn't experience the same degree of success. If you try to cut corners and go the cheaper route, it could happen to you.

- **Be realistic about your workload and lifestyle.**
  Management rights are often promoted as a 'lifestyle' investment, where the work is easy, is often close to the beach and provides a good return. That is true for some complexes, but the reality is that there are only a few where you're well paid and can lead a life of semi-retirement. If you happen to find one of these, that's fantastic, but don't expect it to be the norm. In many cases, you may have to sacrifice some of the income to achieve that sort of lifestyle.

  There isn't a body corporate that's going to pay a manager a large amount of money to do little work. Owners are entitled to expect that the common property is kept clean and tidy, and that the manager is available at reasonable times to deal with management issues. Unit owners begrudge any manager who treats the role as a semi-retirement situation.

A manager has a contract with the body corporate that will specify, in general and/or specific terms, a number of duties. Some of them may be quite time consuming and require the manager's attendance at the complex for specified hours of the day.

When considering a management rights business, a potential buyer should look closely at the size and nature of the complex. This is an important factor to consider when ascertaining the likely amount of time required to keep it in tip-top shape. If you're not able to iron out the details at that time, then make sure you get it done during the course of the purchase. Confirm the office hours and list of duties to calculate roughly how much time it will take to carry them out.

There are two areas that seem to catch buyers up, because they may not initially be mentioned. These are the reception or office hours, and the extent of common property grounds and gardens that have to be looked after. People often fail to appreciate that extensive grounds and gardens do take quite a lot of time to maintain.

See if you can match the likely hours with the remuneration the body corporate is paying. Some buildings have fewer gardens and grounds, and if there are only live-in owners or permanent tenants, the hours might be minimal. Then there are larger buildings where the remuneration allows the manager to engage staff to carry out most or all of the duties, which offers an easier workload. But with a significant investment in the complex, an astute manager is going to want to play some role in the running of the business. Ensuring the team delivers great services and remains productive also requires time and skill on the manager's behalf.

In larger buildings, and even in some smaller ones, a manager wanting the semi-retirement lifestyle can easily engage contractors, such as gardeners or cleaners, to do a lot of the work, with the expense coming out of their own income.

The upside is that when you decide to sell, you can justifiably point out that the true income of the business is higher than you've been receiving, as the work is usually done by a two-person management team.

- **Management rights is a people business.**
A manager must be able to get along with owners, tenants/guests, the body corporate manager and tradespeople in order to run a successful business. Quite simply, if you're not a 'people person', you should probably think twice about going into management rights.

Also, unlike a motel for example, you're not your own boss in all respects. You'll need to be diplomatic in your dealings with the individual(s) who represent the body corporate. As with all business endeavours, it's a good idea to provide win-win solutions and align your interests.

On the other hand, if you're a 'people person' with the capacity to get on with others, while also having the ability to solve rather than escalate problems, you're well placed to succeed in management rights.

- **Managers need to keep good records.**

  Like any business, management rights attracts the good and the bad. Some managers keep poor or distorted records. It's so important—indeed, critical—to have an accountant who understands management rights, in order to carry out the income verification when making the purchase.

  It's equally important to have an accountant with no connection to the seller and is quite happy to rock the boat if they feel the claimed income is dodgy or unsustainable. You need someone who's truly independent and properly representing your interests.

  Some in the industry deliberately discourage buyers from using certain recognised management rights accountants, because they're known for their thoroughness or toughness. A common problem we see, which might only be picked up by an accountant doing their job properly, is not allowing for wages, or enough wages. Some sellers stretch the concept of the amount of work a two-person management team can carry out.

  In addition, you should only select an accountant on the bank's panel, so you can be sure they're experienced, thorough and independent.

  Also remember that there's no guarantee the verified income is what you'll receive. First of all, it's merely the income that the business earned for the period covered by the verification. Depending on how close to the contract date the end of that period was, the income will be some months behind by the time you settle. It's obviously better to make sure the verification period is as close as possible to the date of the contract.

Secondly, the actual gross income received for taxation and other purposes will be somewhere around 10 percent less than the amount verified. That's because the wording in the standard REIQ contract about 'verified net profit' doesn't take into account a number of expenses you'll incur.

Make sure you budget accordingly. A good accountant will be able to help make sure you do, as they won't only verify the income achieved over the relevant period, but will also calculate the likely income going forward and prepare a cash flow projection for you.

There are many more aspects to a financial verification, and your accountant will know exactly what to look out for in that regard.

- **There may be a change of units from the letting pool.**
  Fortunately, history shows that most letting pool numbers remain fairly constant, with any fluctuations being relatively minor. At certain times, though, some managers have found the number of units in their letting pool decreasing as owners cancel letting appointments and move into their units or sell them to owner-occupiers. On the flip side, the letting pool may increase when owners move out and an investor buys the unit.

  The multiplier upon which a management rights business is purchased should reflect the risks of buying the business. And it's important to factor in the change of units from the letting pool, particularly in the case of small-to-medium-sized permanent complexes, where the past trend seemed to be more pronounced. The purchase contract includes a clause that allows negotiation reduction/increase in the purchase price, where the number of units in the letting pool changes after the contract is signed.

How can buyers protect themselves? By investigating the purchase thoroughly. Management rights are sold on the basis of past income levels.

To mitigate the risk, ask the current manager and/or get the accountant who does the verification of financial records to find out how many units were in the letting pool at the beginning, during and end of the year, so you can see the trend and find out the reason for any changing trends.

As the buyer, you should assess the likelihood of more owner/occupiers and if the units are large, spacious and in a good area, or too small for the average owner/occupier. Generally, complexes in noisy locations such as near a major road or train line, will attract tenants rather than owner-occupiers.

These risks should be factored into the purchase price, and the agent and current manager need to be informed about them. Make sure you ask for a condition in the contract that allows for negotiation of the purchase price if the number of units in the letting pool at settlement is less than the requisite level.

- **Research previous disputes.**
  Disputes with the body corporate, or the individual(s) that represent it, can be stressful and debilitating for the resident manager. They can also be expensive to resolve. On the other

hand, complexes with past disputes may represent an opportunity for you to turn the situation to your advantage.

As a general rule, if there was a conflict with the previous manager, it's important to find out the reason for it. If you're at all suspicious, you should make enquiries to ascertain the state of harmony in the complex.

Research the most likely reason(s) for past disputes. Sometimes they arise out of a personality conflict or poor performance by the manager, while at other times they're due to unreasonable expectations on the part of a certain owner.

Before going to contract to purchase a business, investigate the state of harmony within a complex. Because of our extensive exposure to the industry over the years, we at Mahoneys are often aware of the existence of, and reasons for, past disputes. This experience and knowledge can greatly assist buyers in dealing with actual or perceived problems in a complex.

I've talked about the importance of potential new managers having the personality to successfully operate a management rights business. Conversely, those with the wrong personality, who don't like dealing with people, are likely to wind up in conflict with owners and committee members. It's not surprising then that many of the disputes we handle can be traced back to the performance or attitude of the manager.

Where this is the case, these problematic complexes represent an opportunity for an experienced (and even a not-so-experienced) hard-working manager to turn the situation around to their advantage.

But if the investigation reveals that the cause of past disputes or current disharmony is the fault of disruptive owners, you would need to be confident that you could handle the situation in a way that won't damage the business.

While a capable manager with the right people skills can convince owners to oppose the election of a committee member or chairperson who's dictatorial or unreasonable, a complex with a poor history of disputes should be properly researched and considered before being purchased.

- **Know how to avoid and deal with disputes.**
In terms of conflicts, the basic rule is to avoid them in the first place. Of course, this isn't always possible, but there are a few ways all managers can limit conflict.

One of the most important things to do is to constantly reinforce to your owners, particularly investor owners, what a great job you're doing. It can be communicated through your newsletters or a brief flyer with your monthly statements. Investor owners aren't in the building to notice it, and residence owners may not realise the great job you're doing, as everyone is busy living their life nowadays.

Send some photos of the complex or of their unit if you've replaced furnishings or fittings. Tell owners how good your occupancy levels are in comparison to others. Let them know what you've been doing in relation to marketing, what major items of work you're undertaking and how much effort you're putting into them. One manager I knew in a permanent complex made sure he was always in the garden from seven to nine a.m. and four to six p.m., as that was when the owners were leaving for, or coming home from, work. You need to be seen as hard-working so people can appreciate your effort.

It's important to make sure that the owners are aware that you, as manager and not the committee, are the one responsible for the way the complex is presented, as well as all positive changes. Take charge of as much as you can to avoid having committee members usurp your authority. You want owners to think you have your finger on the pulse of the complex, and you're the one who makes things happen. One day you'll need the owners' support, and you want them to be on your side.

Actively seek out the ones who appreciate what you do for committee positions. Lobby them to vote for the nominations you know will cooperate with you and do what's in the best interests of the complex. There's no restriction on lobbying owners to vote in a certain way.

If conflicts do arise, get on top of them straight away. Don't let them fester. Approach the person(s) concerned, and talk the issues through. Be careful not to go on the attack, unless the circumstances demand it. Remain calm and rational.

Be totally familiar with the content of your agreements, and make sure you're doing everything that's required of you. Get any registers in place, including master keys and service contractors such as fire safety and the lifts. Make sure you have all necessary systems in place. If your agreement doesn't have a schedule setting out daily, weekly and monthly duties, make one up yourself, and stick to it. Don't give your opponents any opportunity to find valid fault with what you're doing or not doing. So many managers I speak with have almost no real idea of the extent of the duties required of them under their agreements.

Go through the committee minutes carefully to address all issues that relate to management. Use them as a checklist to make sure you take care of all the duties the committee is expecting you to accomplish.

Document everything that could be contentious. Send emails to confirm issues you've discussed or instructions you received where there's a possibility for confusion or misunderstanding in the future.

If your agreement provides for the body corporate to have a nominated representative that liaises with you, make sure one is appointed. That way you only have to deal with one person and not a group of people with perhaps conflicting ideas about what you should be doing. If your agreement doesn't provide for a single liaison, ask the committee to appoint one anyhow for efficiency and accountability purposes.

Make a point of having regular walks around the complex with the committee representative, so the two of you can identify together any issues that should be addressed, whether it's a one-off problem or something that needs ongoing attention.

Remember that your owners are your clients. Treat them with respect and diplomacy. Listen to their concerns and complaints, show them empathy when justified and firmly, but politely, tell them if you don't share their view.

If there's a dispute, it's really important to get to the root cause of it.

Look closely at your own performance. Are you really doing all that's required of you under your agreement? Review your duties carefully. Don't just assume you're doing everything.

One of the biggest problems we see is the huge gap in expectations of the manager and the unit owners. You can't blame owners for expecting you to do a fair amount of work for the money they pay you. They want you to earn your salary.

Compare how your complex looks to others. Get someone independent to inspect how you're keeping it up. Be prepared to do some critical self-analysis.

If you think the expectations of the committee are too high, or that they don't understand the true nature of your duties, get some advice from an independent expert and look at the ABMA Code that clearly sets out what your duties entail. If it confirms what you believe, suggest to the committee that they meet with this person and/or review the relevant parts of the Code, so they understand the true extent of your duties.

However, if you decide that perhaps your performance is the cause of the problem, you're in the best position to do something about it.

If you're certain that the real issue isn't your performance, you need to work out if the hostility towards you is just one person, a small minority, or the committee, or unit owners in general. Properly assess the extent of the unit owners' ill feelings. It may be that there's just one person who's the dominant cause of the problems. It's amazing how often one individual can poison the attitude of a committee, or even the unit owners.

Here are the questions to ask yourself:
- Is it a personality conflict?
- Could I be the cause of that conflict?
- What, if anything, can I do to resolve/avoid that conflict?

Determine if the person or persons with whom there's a conflict are likely to want to resolve it or if their position/ideas are so entrenched, and their attitude towards you so hostile, that there's little or no point in trying to reason with them. There will be situations where you know either from past dealings with the individual(s) in question, or because of the nature of the individual(s) is so obvious, that there's no chance at all of succeeding, and you shouldn't attempt to resolve it on your own.

Assuming you conclude that the conflict is one that can be resolved, how you do that will depend on what the principal aim is.

If the number one priority is the preservation and/or extension of your agreements, as well as maintenance of the value of your business so you can sell it, then focus on solving any dramatic conflict without escalation. Also be prepared to compromise, so you can sell and move on.

If the priority is to improve your working and living environment, you need to focus on resolving the conflict in a sustainable way, where you and the body corporate have a good ongoing working relationship. That may necessitate some form of legal action on your part.

Where the conflict is caused by one or more committee members such as a dictatorial chairperson, you may decide that the conflict can only be resolved by removing the member(s) from the committee. This can be done with the support of those lot owners who share your concerns about the cause of the conflict.

If 25 percent of lot owners request an EGM to remove one or more committee members, it must be held within forty-two days to consider the motion(s) to do so. This is a tactic many managers have been able to implement to bring reasonableness and fairness back into their relationship with the body corporate.

Once you decide on your goal, work out how you're going to handle it, and take action. I'm not suggesting that dealing with these problems is easy. It can be difficult and stressful. That's why it's important to do all you can to make sure they don't arise in the first place.

### How did you get into the management rights industry?

A firm I was working for was handling a dispute matter for some on-site managers on the Gold Coast, and one of my partners said it looked like a good industry to be involved in, so we learned more about it and then made a name for ourselves in the industry.

### Why did you pick this niche?

It was of interest to me because I've always done property work and management rights, but this seemed more interesting than straight property. We saw it was going to be a growing industry, so we figured it was worthwhile getting involved.

### You have multiple locations in Brisbane, as well as on the Gold Coast. How do you ensure your services are consistent?

All of our office systems are centralised in Brisbane, so the people on the Gold Coast are really working through our systems there. The staff have been trained in the same way. My partner on the Gold Coast, Matthew, was with Michael Clarke for many years before he became lawyer. We then arranged for him to move to the Gold Coast and run the practice down there. Because Matt has been brought up through the firm, he shares our ideals and values and understands the systems.

### What is your firm's biggest goal?

To continue with the steady growth that began when I formed it and consolidate our position in the industry, particularly in regard to management rights.

### What does a typical workday look like for you?

I arrive at the office at somewhere between five and six a.m. and work through until between five or six p.m.

I use the first part of the day before the emails come through and the phone starts ringing, to get through the paperwork. By nine a.m., I've spent a lot of my time responding to emails, dealing with staff and giving them the rundown of their duties. It's not until late afternoon when I can once again deal with other pressing issues.

### What's the most important piece of advice anyone has ever given you?

That's a really interesting question. Honestly, I've had to forge my own way in terms of management rights. Even when I was setting up my law practice, nobody helped me. But through my own observations, I can say it's really important to provide clients with good service and not to focus on the fees.

### What advice would you give to someone thinking about growing their management rights?

Delegating is important, so make sure you have good staff around you. They need to be trained well, so there's consistency in the quality of the service you're delivering.

It's also important to market your product. The short-term managers who do well are those with good marketing expertise and aren't afraid to get creative.

For long-term managers, you need to build a good relationship with your owner. Don't ask how you can do less and get paid more, but how you can give your owners more to make sure they appreciate what you do which will help you in the long term.

### What is your top tip that will inspire your team to perform at their best?

Lead by example. Always communicate with them and encourage them. When they do something good, let them know, and if they make a mistake, talk to them about it in an encouraging way. Make sure you spend some downtime with them as well, so that you get to know each other and build relationships with them.

## What marketing strategies have worked for you?

The number one marketing strategy we've undertaken in recent times is that we're reaching out to our Chinese clients to get help translate our newsletters, articles and information on our website.

Those in the Chinese community seem to know about us but have two major concerns: we don't speak their language and we're too expensive. The message we want to get out there in the marketplace is that the language barrier has never proved to be a problem. And that going to a cheaper lawyer costs them more in the long run, as they wind up having to pay us to fix whatever they did wrong, or their issue can no longer be resolved.

Another great marketing strategy we incorporated is that we maintain regular contact with people in the industry, because you can get isolated if you work from nine to six. This means everyone's making a conscious effort to engage more on a personal level. Though many companies rely on the internet and social media, I just don't think that's necessarily going to help. We get our name out there through our regular newsletters and magazine articles. We believe that the more you engage with those in the industry, the more likely you are to receive referrals.

## What were some of the mistakes you made in the first year of starting your own firm?

Well, I've effectively started my own firm twice now, and if I made mistakes, it probably had to do with not focusing enough initially on the overhead. It's much easier to make and spend money than it is to save money, so you must be careful where you spend it. What you pay in overhead comes out of your pocket, so I think keeping an eye on it is an important part of running your own business.

The other mistake I made perhaps initially was that I didn't utilise modern technology to its full extent, so it took a while to get to our top efficiency.

Other than that, we tried not to make too many mistakes and wound up doing pretty well.

**How did you make your first million?**
The thing about being a lawyer is that you only get paid for the time and effort you put in, and there's only a certain number of hours in the day. Since you charge per hour, you're limited as to what you can make in a law practice.

However, if you hire staff who are also billing out at an hourly rate and are producing excellent work, you can do well as a lawyer. The challenge is to make sure you look after those people and retain them, and we've been fortunate enough to have been able to do that.

**What motivates and drives you to get up early every day and go to work?**
I love my work and the people I work with. One employee has been with me for many years. I'm keen to ensure that when I retire, I can enjoy my life.

I also have a number of children who are fully or partly dependent upon me so that's pretty good motivation.

**Do you continue to practice your personal development? If so, please share some of your strategies.**
It's not surprising that lawyers now have one of the highest suicide rates of any profession in Australia, and it's all due to the stress they work under.

Reading books that help me understand humanity, exercising, and in general looking after myself physically and mentally, are great ways to deal with the stress that comes with running busy practice. A good diet is also important.

I just finished reading the book *Sapiens*, which is about the history of humankind and am now reading the sequel, *Homo Deus*, which is about the future of humanity.

## What do you believe are the essential qualities of being successful in business?

You have to be careful who you trust, provide a product that's better than your opposition, while at the same time, placing your customers first. You also need to under-promise and over-deliver.

## What do you think stops people from being successful in the management rights industry?

There are people who don't have the right personality for the industry because they can't deal with difficult people. They're unable to appreciate what they've bought and so don't understand the reasonable expectations of their owners, which is that they actually have to put in work for the reward that the body corporate pays them.

I mean, it's not that difficult a business to run if you understand what's expected. Again, I think it comes back to service.

## How do you connect with friends?

Going to the golf course is my favourite; but also by telephone, emails and trying to get together with them whenever I can. I don't use Facebook or Twitter.

### How do you deal with a troublesome team member?
I try and understand what's bothering them, so I don't make any assumptions. Then I work out the available options to deal with the issue, based on if it's a personal- or work-related.

### How do you handle problematic clients?
I think you have to be patient with troublesome clients and have a good strategy of dealing with them. Again, listening to their issue and having some patience is the key. Then try and find some of the parts you agree with. This takes all the angst out of the conversation, which helps them calm down, so you can better get your point across.

Most people are reasonable. But whether their issue is justified or not, it's important to be patient and solicitous, so you can understand where they're coming from and try to find some common ground.

### How do you develop new relationships?
I guess when you've reached a certain age, you've formed a lot of personal relationships, so it's not as though you're out there making a whole lot of new ones. It's really just a matter of taking people as you find them and being yourself. If you happen to click, then the relationship will build from there. I usually don't deliberately go out of my way to build relationships with people. If it happens, it happens.

I think when you're younger it might be different, but as you get older, you learn to appreciate the important things in life, so you're looking for those who have the same common denominator, and it happens naturally.

As far as business is concerned, I'm naturally enthusiastic about what I do and about management rights, so I'm always happy to share my ideas with people who are interested and am open to that being the beginning of a great business relationship.

**What challenges do you sometimes come across in your relationships?**
I think some people are confined to seeing things from their own perspective and have a fixed view. They believe their opinion is the only right one, and everybody else is wrong. This means, at times, they're unable to take the focus off themselves and look at the broader picture, so it's always a challenge to work out a way of dealing with them.

## The seven wisdoms from this chapter:

1. You need to have the right kind of personality to succeed in management rights.

2. Always find out the reason for past conflicts.

3. Constantly reinforce to your owners, particularly investor owners, what a great job you're doing.

4. If conflicts do arise, get on top of them straight away. Don't let them fester.

5. Delegating is important, so make sure you have good, well-trained staff around you, so there's consistency in the quality of the service you're delivering.

6. Be careful who you trust, provide a product that's better than your opposition, put your customers first and under-promise and over-deliver.

7. Your owners are your clients. Treat them with respect and diplomacy. Listen to their concerns and complaints, show them empathy when justified and firmly but politely tell them if you don't share their view.

# FREE GIFT

John has generously offered the readers of *The Management Rights Formula* a free forty-five-minute initial consultation on any management rights or body corporate matter, valued at $500. Get your bonus by registering now via **www.mrformula.com.au/bonus**.

# CHAPTER SEVEN
# Scott Lai, CPA

## Keep What You Make: Asset Protection and Smart Tax Strategies

*" Accounting is the language of business."*
~Warren Buffett

Scott Lai was born in Fujian Province, China, and graduated from Griffith University in Australia with a master's degree in Accounting.

In 2010, Scott founded Q&T Accountants, which is a registered tax agency and professional accounting firm certified by CPA Australia and is currently the largest Chinese accounting firm specialising in management rights.

Scott is also the director of JSY Capital, which is one of a few non-retail professional funds management companies that holds an Australia Financial Service License.

JSY Capital's business scope includes, but is not limited to, private equity funding, investment portfolio management, lending products and fixed income products.

## What is Q&T Accountants?

Q&T Accountants is a CPA-certified accounting practice and tax agency that's been providing services to the management rights industry since 2008. We have two offices, one in Brisbane and another on the Gold Coast, with a total of twenty-five full-time employees.

We provide a wide range of services, such as bookkeeping, preparation and lodgement of periodic activity statements and preparation of financial reports, as well as tax consulting and assistance with tax returns.

We specialise in management rights, and our income verification reports are recognised by a number of major banks in Australia.

## What services do you provide to clients?

1. **Advice and Analysis**
   We provide advice and analysis of the ideal entity structure based on our sophisticated experience and knowledge of the management right industry.

2. **Income Verification Report**
   We're able to conduct an on-site income verification for the purchaser of a management right business, which has proven to be useful when financing is required at the time of acquisition.

3. **Business Compliance Services**
   We provide business compliance services, such as bookkeeping, periodic GST and PAYG reporting, annual financial reports and income tax return preparation. We also provide other services like trust account audit, tax planning and assistance with a bank loan review or refinance.

> **"** In this world nothing can be said to be certain, except death and taxes. **"**
> ~**Benjamin Franklin**

**What should people consider when starting a management rights business and setting up the appropriate structure?**

How you pay taxes is one of the most important factors you need to take into consideration prior to signing a contract and setting up a business structure.

A scalable structure has the best long-term benefits and reflects what your needs are in regard to your business objective. The main question is: *who* you would like to collaborate with?

When you own a management right business, you receive a highly stable income due to the fixed body corporate salary, leasing commissions, management fees and other service incomes. But you might wonder how the structure is taxed on its profit and the way you can maximise the tax deduction. Everything hinges on the company structure.

## What structures should management rights buyers consider?

1. **Trust**

    A trust allows you to have control over your own tax planning, asset protection and distribution of wealth. There are two types of trusts: the unit trust and the family trust, and the structure can be either simple or complex, depending on the size of the business and the prospect of development.

    - **Family Trust**

        A family trust is a discretionary trust that's set up to hold a family's assets or to run a business. It often involves spouses, children or parents. Members of the family trust are taxed at different rates, depending on their income proportion. A flexible tax planning strategy can minimise the tax payable by streaming distributions to beneficiaries at the lowest individual marginal tax rates. This means a trust's capital gains and franked distributions can be streamed to beneficiaries for tax purposes by making these beneficiaries specifically entitled to the amounts specified.

    - **Unit Trust**

        A unit trust is where the rights of the beneficiaries (unit holders) to income and capital are fixed. It's unitised and divided amongst the beneficiaries based on the number of units they're holding. This structure is suitable for unrelated members from two or more separate families.

        The trust pays tax on behalf of certain beneficiaries, and all incomes must be distributed.

2. **Company**

   A company pays 27.5–30 percent tax on its profits according to the turnover of the business. This structure requires that the business is run independently, and there are no beneficiaries living in Australia.

3. **Trust + Company**

   Having a company as a trustee is also a popular structure as it has all the advantages of the trust structure, while the assets are held under the trustee's name. It separates the private assets of individual trustees and protects the ownership of them when the death of the director or trustee of the company occurs.

> " The secret to success is to own nothing, but control everything."
> ~Nelson Rockefeller

## What's the best structure if the plan is to buy a management rights valued at less or more than two million dollars?

Having a trust with a corporate trustee structure is highly recommended if you intend to buy a management right business valued at under two million dollars. If you've owned a small business for more than twelve months, you may be eligible to get the benefit of the small business active assets reduction on capital gain. According to the Australian Taxation Office (ATO), the definition of a small business is one that has an annual revenue turnover (excluding GST) of less than two million dollars.

If you're buying a management rights valued at over two million dollars, a company structure is more suitable than a trust, because the annual turnover rate is higher, and it's more difficult to make a distribution to your family member based on profit. Right now, the current tax rate for individual taxation income above $90,000 is 37 percent, and $180,000 is 45 percent. Paying the corporate tax rate of 27.5–30 percent is a better option to maximise your tax benefit.

### What's the best structure if someone plans to buy more than one management rights business?

If you're considering buying more than one management rights businesses, then you can choose either a company or trust structure. The main consideration is how to attribute the profit effectively and maximise the tax deduction at the same time, when two high profitable management rights are purchased under the same name and entity.

If there aren't enough units or family members to classify the high income, the person who undertakes the distribution will have to pay a higher income tax. The supreme tax rate is 41.51 percent for the individual who has a taxable income of over $180,000. The second consideration is financial. If each management right business you're planning to buy has its own bank lender, then you should have an entity linked to each one, rather than one entity handling both. This will help with organisation and management.

### What are some of the common mistakes people make in setting up the structure?

One of the common mistakes is not considering the potential personal risks. Business buyers tend to forget the possible impact on their personal and family assets. They might be directly affected by the wrong structure as soon as their business runs into trouble.

Keep in mind that it's important to have legal documents when it comes to managing a corporation. All corporations should have an agreement declaring the rights, responsibility, financial contributions, distribution of rewards and provisions for separating interest when there are any changes of circumstance for all parties involved.

### What information do you expect to obtain from the income verification report?

After you sign the contract and have purchased a management right business, the first important step is to do an income verification.

Accountants have an important role in both the purchase of management rights and the ongoing support once you've bought your business.

One of the benefits of buying management rights is the formal verification of net profit conducted by an accountant prior to completing your purchase.

This is your opportunity to have an independent expert examine the books and records of the business and verify the net profit represented to you. If the variance of net operating profit between your accountant's estimate and the vendor's figures is significant, it could affect your final business contract price or even break the contract.

This process can be carried out with accuracy, as management rights is a business that works on a trust account. The income and expenses are able to be traced by those who know what to look for. As management rights specialists, Q&T Accountants conducts over three hundred trust account audits each year. We're familiar with the various types of software used for trust account managing and are therefore able to verify the incomes from trust accounts, regardless of how complex they are.

The verification report is completed early in the due diligence process, which is usually fourteen days after the contract is signed.

If you wish to choose an accountant to perform the income verification for you, please contact us immediately after the contract is signed. We will try our best to complete the verification within the time frame.

**What ongoing service does an accountant provide once the purchase of management rights has been completed?**

- Auditing of the trust account in accordance with the requirements of the Agents Financial Administration Act of 2014.
- Preparation of financial statements and income tax returns for your business.
- Assistance with setting up books and records for the trust and general account.
- Attending to registration with the taxation office for a group tax in cases where there are employees.
- Assistance with workers' compensation, superannuation and other statutory registration,

> *Risk comes from not knowing what you are doing.*
> ~Warren Buffett

## What's the most important aspect of a management rights purchase that someone can easily overlook?

The most overlooked aspect when purchasing management rights is trust account auditing.

The licensee needs to lodge Agents Financial Administration Form 5 to the Office of Fair Trading (OFT) within two months after opening a trust account, in accordance with Sections 11, 13 and 17 of the Agents Financial Administration Act of 2014.

The licensee also needs to appoint an auditor within one month after opening a trust account and give written notice to the Office of Fair Trading within one month after the appointment of an auditor. In some cases, the purchasing process may take more than a couple of months, so the bank will open the trust account for the new manager at an early stage of the process. According to the regulations, even if there aren't any transactions and the business hasn't been in operation, the licensee still needs to lodge Form 5 and appoint an auditor within the time frame regulated by the Act.

## What are the requirements for a bank reconciliation?

The bank statement lists the activity in the bank account during the recent month, as well as the balance in the bank account.

You need to verify that the amounts on the bank statement are consistent or compatible with the amounts in your cash account in your general ledger, and vice versa. This process of confirming the amounts is referred to as a bank reconciliation.

The OFT requires that the bank reconciliation must use the closing balance as of the last day of the month, and the timing of the trust account cash book reconciliation should be conducted in accordance with regulation 17 of the Agents Financial Administration Regulation 2014 (AFAR 2014), which states that the principal agent must reconcile the trust account cash book balance within five business days after the end of each month.

This means you need to start the process at the beginning of the next month to ensure you've received all rental payments up until end of the previous month. For some software, you may need to manually change the date back to the last day of the previous month when you do the reconciliation.

## What do you recommend to simplify the compliance requirements?

Using a computerised accounting system can make it easier to comply with many of the requirements of the Act and Regulations.

The best way to do this is by using industry-acceptable software to manage the trust account, such as HiRUM. Microsoft Word and Excel are not accepted by the OFT, as the records of the previous period can easily be changed.

If an agent uses a computerised accounting system to manage their trust account records, they must ensure that:

- it doesn't allow the deletion of a trust ledger account, unless the balance is zero and a record of the account is kept immediately before it's deleted

- any amendments to a transaction are recorded on the system as a separate transaction in chronological order
- the system has enough backup capability to record the information required by the Act
- the system is backed up at least once a month
- backed-up information isn't stored at the agent's business address and is protected from anything that could affect it such as magnetic interference.

**How do you record payments?**
The agent must record the transaction and issue a trust account receipt to the payer when they receive cash or cheque payments. The cash or cheque must then be deposited to the trust account on the same or next business day.

**What is a rental bond?**
A rental bond, or security deposit, is money paid by the tenant at the start of a tenancy agreement and is used as financial protection by the lessor against the tenant breaching the terms of the agreement.

**What's the procedure for lodging rental bonds?**
A rental bond is lodged with the Residential Tenancies Authority (RTA) online, or by post, using a Bond Lodgement (Form 2) within ten days after the bond arrives at the trust account.

Some agents delay lodging the Form 2, because they're waiting for the tenants to sign it. However, this is not a good excuse for a late lodgement. They need to lodge the Form 2 without the tenant's signatures and then do it again after it's signed.

## As an accountant, what do you think about management rights?

Management rights is a simple business that generally has a good return on investment, as it brings in a stable income and has limited costs.

If it's a small business, then it can be operated by one or two people. The management rights model can apply to long- and short-term letting. Long-term letting includes student accommodation and residential tenancies. Short-term includes holiday letting, corporate letting, groups and conferences. Of the two, long-term letting is easier to manage.

Good timing and excellent financial management leads to success in this industry. As long as the company has its cost under control, it will have a higher income return. This is because you don't need to manage inventory or worry about shop renting problems. You can achieve a high stable income with flexible working hours.

Short-term letting is different from long-term letting and can be more financially rewarding if you're experienced in the field or willing to work with the experts in this book to acquire the skills. It's similar to a small hotel system. You have responsibilities for keeping your services and accommodation at a good standard, which means more staff, more time and more costs.

## What are some of the best ways to increase income within the management rights industry?

The best way to increase income is to provide multiple services in one business.

You can take all subcontracting jobs, such as gardening or repairing works, if you have relevant licenses or qualifications, as these provide more potential income.

Furthermore, building up good relationships with people is important in the management rights business. For instance, if you've been managing one of the properties efficiently for a few years, and you've built up a good relationship with the owner, they might allow you to be their property agent. This means you can earn a commission when you sell their property. Meanwhile, you can keep the letting property for investment purposes, which prevents a loss from an outsider agent or avoids it being converted to being owner-occupied.

## Seven wisdoms from this chapter:

1. Prior to signing a contract, plan how much tax you'll need to pay, and understand which business structure is best for you.

2. If you're thinking of growing your management rights portfolio, make sure to use a scalable structure.

3. Business buyers tend to forget the possible impact on their personal and family assets, and might be directly affected by the wrong structure as soon as their business runs into trouble.

4. Personal risk can be minimised and your assets protected by utilising the right structure.

5. Have a management rights accountant on the bank's panel verify the net income.

6. Find the management rights you want to buy, and then engage an accountant who's an expert in management rights.

7. The best way to increase income is to provide multiple services within one business.

# FREE GIFT

Scott is providing the readers of *The Management Rights Formula* a great bonus consultation session, valued at over $395, that will help you set up the correct structure to protect your assets and legally save you from paying excessive taxes. With the tools and processes provided in this consultation session, you can save millions.

To claim your awesome gift, visit **www.mrformula.com.au/bonus**.

# CHAPTER EIGHT

# Richard Skiba & Jessica Dong

## Management Rights Super Exit Strategy: The Fast and Simple Way to Sell Your Business at the Highest Price

> *SIRE enhances the well-being of your management rights business, helps you satisfy the stakeholders and assists you in supporting your local communities.*
> ~The SIRE Team

After winning the Best Electronic Design award for developing a laser detection system in high school, Richard began his career in the electrical industry with Powerlink Queensland as an EHV Metering Accuracy Analyst. In this capacity, he reported on the accuracy of the revenue and check metering systems to NEMMCO. He then moved on to Australia's national communications regulator, Australia Communications and Media Authority (ACMA), as a radiocommunications and telecommunications inspector.

During his ten years in the workforce, Richard explored many opportunities in various industries and decided that contributing to the management rights industry would provide an excellent income combined with a great work-family-life balance.

Today, through his management rights sales agency, Richard has helped thousands of people explore new opportunities to increase their income, optimise their operations, create wealth and achieve their goals, regardless of where they've come from, their present situation or where they want to go. His only regret is not getting into management rights earlier.

## What does SIRE Management Rights do?

SIRE stands for Synergy International Real Estate. We help management rights owners sell their business for the highest price and in the quickest way possible by simplifying the process.

Our motto is *Synergy Though Sharing Experience, Knowledge and Strategies*. And most importantly, we take systemised daily actions to achieve intended results.

## What is SIRE's mission?

To be the preferred sales specialist for management rights owners, as well as trusted advisors to help our clients build their business and live the lifestyle they deserve.

## Do you personally invest in management rights?

Yes. The SIRE team members are all actively invested in management rights, which helps us share up-to-date solutions with our clients, while also demonstrating that we truly believe in the products we're selling.

## What's the advantage of using the SIRE team to sell management rights?

First of all, you'll get a higher price. But more importantly, it's a complex business transaction, quite different from residential, commercial or land sales. This is because there are so many conditions that need to be met with numerous stakeholders and legislation involved in the contract. You really need a specialised expert who understands management rights from a commercial, operational and systemised point of view, and how the body corporate operates in order to ensure a smooth transition. This requires a team behind you who can warn you of possible complications and provide amicable solutions where all parties' interests are protected.

It might sound complicated, but we've had a 100 percent body corporate approval rate since the day we opened, so it's second nature to us.

> *If you think hiring a professional is expensive, wait till you hire an amateur.*
> ~**Red Adair**

**How can someone avoid crashing the contract?**
This is a true art form. You have to be familiar with the process and also be a great negotiator to achieve a settlement. For instance, you need to know:

- the stakeholders' interest in the transition
- the management rights business you're selling
- the motivation behind why the seller wants to sell
- why the buyer wants to purchase a particular management rights business
- where the roadblocks are and how to deal with them before they arise
- how to build rapport and trust, so all parties are working toward the same outcome at the same time
- how the bank, valuer and committee work
- how to prepare for the body corporate interview
- how to educate the buyers and sellers about the process, including why and how it's done
- how to co-ordinate a team of management rights specialised service providers.

The SIRE Team has been systemising the whole process by refining and improving it daily. Our system is dynamic and consistently produces smooth settlements. We're dedicated to providing the best service. And the best part is that we love the process.

**What should someone look for when engaging a broker to sell their management rights?**
You should find someone with a great track record in settlement who understands the importance of confidentiality. They should also have great negotiation and marketing skills backed by a genuine enthusiasm. And most importantly, they need to specialise in management rights.

At SIRE, we pride ourselves on being enthusiastic experts in management rights transactions. The SIRE Team loves what they do and really believes in what they're selling. We're also head and shoulders above the competition. This may sound like a cliché, but it's so true.

We see so many buildings transformed, which helps make a better community for the residents, a great livelihood for the managers and increases the business value. This is what really drives the SIRE Team to work harder for our clients. We speak from the heart and are honest about the benefits of each business.

We're dedicated to remaining positive and always seeing the solution.

**What recommendations would you give to someone selling their management rights?**
Get organised, and call the SIRE Team to assess your business. We can provide you with some simple tips to implement that will improve the value of your business. Or you can go to **www.mrformula.com.au/sell.html** to

download the essential documents that will help you get your information organised before selling your management rights business.

> *There is no magic bullet. It's about having the right team and great market exposure.*
> ~The SIRE Team

**What's the most important thing you've learned about successful management rights/business deals?**
Understand with whom you are working.

Armed with this knowledge, you can lead your clients to make the right decisions, the sale will be solid and you'll have contributed to their quality of life.

The essence of our business is to help our clients achieve their goals and realise their dreams. This is why our entire sales method is less demanding, the transition processes are smoother and our clients are more successful.

**What are SIRE's plans and goals for the next ten years?**
We've achieved the goals we set nearly a decade ago for the agency and our team, and we're confident that we'll accomplish any key milestones we set in the future. When I look back at the key decision to focus on Queensland's management rights industry, I believe it was our best option at the time, given the superior legislative framework and regulations that govern Queensland's management rights industry.

As for our future, we will continue to focus on Queensland's management rights industry, because we know it well, and that's where the buyers, investors and operators want to purchase at this point in time. We're expanding our management rights sales interstate and internationally, and are prepared to launch our company where we believe it's viable and profitable.

To achieve this expansion of the agency, we will persistently continue with every team member's personal development and training and continue to adopt the best practices. To join The SIRE Team, go to **www.mrformula.com.au/team**.

### How does The SIRE Team determine their success?

Measuring our success is first done internally. We set the goals we want to achieve, both individually and as a whole team, and define the results in detail as to when, where and how we're going to execute our actions.

SIRE's core focus is selling management rights businesses. The key measure of our success is our personal growth, helping our clients and the number of sales we close.

The high calibre of the clients we work with has taught us so much about the business, such as having the right mindset and making sure to keep networking and leading by example. This is so we can continue to improve each day, even if it's just by one percent.

Our success is measured by helping our clients improve these five areas in their lives:

- relationships
- personal growth and spirituality

- lifestyle
- health
- wealth

**How do you go that extra mile for your clients?**
We encourage our clients to think like entrepreneurs and have a long-term vision of building a highly saleable business from the day they settle their purchase. We really understand their needs, issues and desires, and use all the resources at our disposal to solve their problems and fulfil their aspirations.

We assist our clients with being more efficient, so they're recharged and ready to outperform themselves on a daily basis. We inspire them to fine-tune their marketing or website, improve their occupancy rate and share solutions. We let them know we understand how they feel about the kinds of unique situations on-site managers experience. But we always remember to have fun at the same time.

We're open to sharing everything we've learned with our clients, and you're welcome to join us. Please go to **www.mrformula.com.au/event** to find out the details of our workshops and events.

**What is your best backup?**
Our system and team. By the end of 2016, our client database had grown quite large. To better manage it and provide superior service, the co-founders spent the majority of 2017 travelling around Asia and Australia to learn from the successful entrepreneurs about the latest updates and technology, and refine our daily processes and procedures.

We can now plug anyone into the SIRE system and produce 95 percent of the similar results, as if the number one sales team member was personally servicing the clients, while the remaining 5 percent can be made up by coaching and weekly training.

We're constantly looking for people with a great attitude who love to make a positive impact on others. If you're one of these positively spirited people and want to work in this rewarding industry, please contact us at sales@siremanagementrights.com.au.

## What sets SIRE apart from other management rights brokers?

We empower management rights owners to create a higher income, systemise processes and procedures, and make a positive difference in the strata industry. We get our clients the highest price in the quickest way possible, and we do it better than the competition.

We love learning about new technology and strategies, and put theory into practice. Since 2013, when we started selling management rights, we've conducted in-depth interviews with management rights owners on a daily basis. This process highlighted the differences between good management rights businesses and those that can be improved upon. These are some of the questions we ask to determine how well the business is running:

- Is the manager working daily in or on their business?
- Are there systems in place for consistency and efficiency?
- How are their relationships with their owners?
- What is the level of service they provide to their owners, tenants and residents?
- Who are the experts they do or don't associate with?
- What is their attitude towards their business and relationships?
- What kind of marketing effort do they put into the business?

Once we've compiled this information, we can quickly identify the potential income and areas of improvement. From there we can determine what types of buyers would succeed in this type of business based on their personality, professional background, attitude and financial situation.

**How can someone make their management rights business more attractive to a buyer?**

Buyers will check for the following:

- **Reoccurring income.**
  Buyers like assurance that they will be able to maintain or grow the income from the business.

- **A long agreement length.**
  Buyers like long-term agreements with a lot of time remaining.

- **The duties that need to be performed to ensure continued income.**
  They need to make sure the work will get done and what resources will be needed.

- **The systems in place that will automate the duties as much as possible.**
  Are there systems in place, or will they have to create them?

- **How well the team performs and if the business requires staff.**
  Do they work as a cohesive team to get the work done efficiently?

- **The product (location, room layout, presentation, services, client base) and training that's offered.**
  All things being equal, systemised and well-documented handover training adds value to your business.

The multiplier achieved also depends heavily on the sales specialist you engage to market your management rights.

Over the years, we've fine-tuned the process of getting management rights owners the highest multiplier in the quickest way possible.

## How can someone improve the value of their management rights business?

It's really quite simple. The more reoccurring income/cash flow your business generates, the more value the bank and buyer will place on it. And the easier, more efficient and automated your income is, the higher the multiplier the bank and buyer will place on your income. This means you get the double effect of a higher income and less time spent in the business, which equals more money and freedom.

There are also other factors that will increase the value of your business, such as goodwill, a great team and a training system. Two years ago, I offered a higher price for a business, just because I knew that the training the business operator gave me would be worth $50,000, which is the cost of hiring a business coach.

## Could you give some examples of passive ways to increase income?

Over the years, we've sold many buildings that have an infrastructure in place for the management rights owner to resell electricity or provide electricity meter reading services for a monthly income. I have a background in the power industry, so I absolutely loves this idea. We run an information event each month which covers the following:

1. **How to reduce the body corporate costs for electricity supplied to the common area.**

   These systems provide a cheaper rate to the body corporate for an electricity retailer to supply the power that will energise electrical devices in the common area, including heating, cooling and general consumption.

   If the body corporate can purchase electricity for a lower price, or it can reduce their electrical energy consumption, then the bill will be lower, and therefore the levies will be as well. If the levies are reduced, then you as an owner pay less and will have more money.

   Each building or complex is unique and needs to be analysed to determine where and how the modifications in the electrical supply and billing systems can be implemented to achieve the best results, such as gradually changing the halogen/fluorescent/incandescent lights with LED technology.

   It costs a bit more to purchase initially, but the savings in usage will pay each device off in a year or two, or even less if they're being used heavily. Also, fewer lights will need replacing over time. If you have 261 halogen lights in the common area, and they fail at a rate of 25 percent per year, it equates to more than forty light bulbs/starters/inductors/PFC capacitors per year! This is time and money.

2. **How each unit can offset their own electricity consumption.**

   There are solar electricity systems that save the unit owners money by basically having discounted or even free electricity. As crazy as it sounds, it's real and works nicely for particular types of format plans.

3. **Electrical Distribution Networks**

   There are buildings that have electrical distribution networks and/or metering systems that are owned by the caretaker. These networks and meters are assigned upon purchasing the management rights business.

   Basically, residents are delivered electricity to their units from the electrical distribution frame to the unit, via the electric cabling owned by the caretaker. They will then issue the electricity consumer an invoice to pay on a periodic basis for using the cabling or meters owned by them.

   Another aspect is that if you own the electricity meters in the building, you can perform the meter reading and charge the customer a meter reading fee.

4. **Bulk Electricity Supply Agreements**

   Some buildings are supplied electricity from the street through high-power cables that run through the bulk supply meter. The caretaker has the right to provide electricity to the units in the building. This means they can negotiate a bulk supply agreement with an electricity retailer to purchase their electricity at a low price, say fifteen cents per kWh. The caretaker then supplies electricity to the units in the building at a higher price, for instance twenty cents per kWh.

We're offering all readers of *The Management Rights Formula* an invitation to come to our monthly information session. Also, if you're a manager, make sure to invite all of your owners and investors to this event, which is available over webinar, so anyone from anywhere can attend at the same time. Go to **www.mrformula.com.au/events.html** to register.

## What are some other ways to increase net income?

1. **Increase your letting pool.**
   This is the best way to increase your net income and the sale value of your business. It's something every manager should be working on every day. We've seen some great management rights operators systemise this process, and we share these ideas with our team. Every manager is welcome to attend a free session by going to www.mrformula.com.au/events.

2. **Offer wi-fi internet service to residents.**
   There's an initial outlay to set up the wi-fi network, but once installed, you can charge users a weekly fee.

3. **Provide a vending machine.**
   Usually the machines are supplied and re-stocked by a provider that pays you a percentage of the money put into the machine. Another option is to purchase the vending machine and re-stock it yourself, thus giving you a higher profit margin.

4. **Offer repair and maintenance services.**
   General repairs that don't require a licence or qualification can be done by an experienced handyman. You can have an arrangement where they do the repair and invoice you for the job. Then you issue the owner an invoice with a margin on top of what it costs you.

5. **Offer real estate sales services.**
   When an owner wishes to put their unit up for sale, you can be the one to sell it. You will need to be proficient at sales and have a real estate agent licence to do this. However, the commission is excellent,

particularly if you're selling a unit in your letting pool. This means you can at least get the money back that you paid when you purchased the letting rights.

Another important factor is that you control the unit to stay in the letting pool if the new owner is an investor. In fact, this is so important, it's why we run our workshop. We need to explain all the options, so you can choose the best one that suits your business objective and lifestyle. All information is available at the end of the chapter.

6. **Offer short-term letting if possible.**
   In a mixed short-term and permanent letting building, where they offer good location or niche facilities, and if the unit is fully furnished, then it may be a good idea to switch the letting from long term to shorter term and receive higher rates.

7. **Improve the condition of the accommodation.**
   You can increase the rent or rate you charge and get investors a higher return, so you can get more commission and letting fees. Depending on the owner and their budget, doing simple things like re-painting or laying new carpet can make a difference. It's even better if the owner can afford a new kitchen and bathroom. Have a chat with them well before the tenant's lease ends, as the best time to do the renovation is when the lease finishes, and they vacate the property.

8. **Increase the occupancy rate.**
   Improving the condition of the accommodation will help increase the occupancy rate. Other strategies include adjusting the rent or rates to be more competitive.

For example, a new building in close proximity has just finished construction and offers new features and facilities. Potential tenants and customers will shop around for what they think is the best deal.

When showing a unit to a prospective long-term tenant, ask them what they think about the building and unit, so you can gauge if they like the product you're offering. You then need to ask them what their rent price range is. Get them to make an offer for the unit, and then have a chat with the owner to find out if they're willing to negotiate. Most of the time they are, and now you've leased the apartment and increased the occupancy rate.

The next step is to send a notice to current tenants of a rent increase at least eight weeks before their lease is up. Even if it's five or ten dollars per week, the tenant will usually be okay with this amount as compared to the inconvenience and costs associated with vacating the unit and finding a new place to live.

Another aspect that has an effect on rent/rates is the season. If a particular time of year is slow, a strategy for permanent letting is to negotiate a lease end date to a time of year when there's more market activity. For short-term letting, it may be feasible to change the mode to long term, which means letting in the off-peak seasons to help with the cash flow for you and your owners.

To implement the strategies mentioned here, come to our monthly event. Instead of trying to reinvent the wheel, you'll learn how to fine-tune or make an action plan that's ready to be implemented into your business.

Go to **www.mrfomula.com.au/event** to register.

9. **Improve or change to different marketing channels, portals and partner networks.**

   The first thing you need to do is have a good look at the photos you use to market the unit for rent or sale. Quite frequently, I see photos of units that are taken using a phone or standard camera, and these photos don't help with attracting people to come see the property.

   You need to hire a specialist photographer who uses professional HD cameras, perspective lenses and correct lighting. The differences between the professional and sub-amateur photography are dramatic. We've found that advertising using professional photography achieves more enquiries, higher rent rates and sale prices and lower vacancy rates.

   The good thing about getting a set of professional photos taken is that it costs around $120, which is a mandatory investment that will pay for itself many times over. If any of your owners don't have professional photos for their unit, you need to talk to them about these benefits.

   Another advantage is that with you as their property manager, fewer inspections will be performed before leasing or selling a unit. Other owners will see the quality of your advertising and consider appointing you as well.

   Having professional photos of your owner's unit is half the job. The other half is having a good set of professional photos of the common area facilities and the building. These are your responsibility so make a small one-off investment for your business and get a set of professional photos of the building and the facilities. Don't forget to update your website and marketing portals with your new professional photos!

10. **Reduce your business expenses while maintaining the quality of your services and efficiency.**

    You need to have a look at each expense, which means going through the receipts and invoices one by one. Ideally, this should be handled at least every year. Expenses to investigate include:

    - landline and mobile phones
    - internet
    - website and email hosting
    - electricity
    - motor vehicle
    - insurances
    - account auditing
    - bank fees
    - cleaners
    - gardeners
    - booking systems.

    Just start by reviewing one ongoing expense every month, and then shop around and negotiate a better deal with your supplier. Things like old fax technology is obsolete, so you can cancel it altogether.

11. **Supply gardening services.**

    Some buildings require the residents to maintain their gardens and lawns, particularly with standard format plan buildings. Have a chat with them, and send emails and flyers to inform them of your competitive pricing.

12. **Invoice for cleaning services.**

    You probably already have a contractor that takes care of cleaning inside the units when the tenants or customers vacate. You should also be invoicing the vacating tenants or owners with a profit margin on top of what you pay your cleaners. Again, inform them of your competitive pricing.

13. **Partner up with businesses related to your industry sector**
Align yourself with insurance companies, tourist spots, restaurants and travel providers to offer more competitive services and deliver value to your residents and guests.

Partner up with utility connection companies that arrange the tenant's gas, electricity and internet. There's good money to be made this way, particularly when there are new tenants moving in, and they ask you about the utilities. Just explain that they have the freedom to use any retailer, but you could help with all the connections for free with your concierge service.

14. **Increase the productivity and efficiency of your staff and contractors.**
You should know exactly what your team is doing and how long it takes them to perform their tasks, as well as the expected results. For instance, if there's a task your team member is currently performing that takes a substantial amount of their time, you may need to consider retraining or outsourcing that particular task to a dedicated specialist who can do it quicker and cheaper.

## What is the main reason managers don't take action to improve their income, and how can they overcome it?

Most managers know ways to increase their income, but many are reluctant to take the key steps in order to get the results they want.

The biggest reason is that they feel they don't have the time to implement these strategies due to their day-to-day workload or constant distractions. In our office, we play a game called 'Did I win, or did the distraction win?'

I have a four-step plan for getting tasks done in half the time:

- **Step One**
  Make a list of all the tasks you do on a daily basis.

- **Step Two**
  Prioritise your list to make sure the tasks that make the most impact on your business are at the top.

- **Step Three**
  Systemise the reoccurring tasks. Figure out which ones can be done at certain times of the day. For example, taking the general waste bulk bins in the evening.

- **Step Four**
  Turn off all distractions. Slice your time into twenty-minute blocks, and get on with finishing the task at hand.

Once you're efficient at doing a task, time yourself, and make a training video for your staff. Then you have the option of continuing to do the task yourself or delegating it, so you can focus on income-increasing activities.

**How can someone improve the value of their business?**
I'd like to share with you a simple seven-step process that will improve the value of your business. One important thing to remember is that you want a fair exchange. In other words, the only reason you should get paid more is because you provide more value to your clients and customers. Then they will be your raving fans, and your business will thrive. Here are the seven simple steps that will get you on the road to increasing the value of your business:

- **Step One: Go through your pre-sale profit-and-loss statement.** Brainstorm ways to reduce your costs and improve all aspects of your business.

  If you've been with the SIRE Team all along, you should be pleased, as we always work together to improve your business worth on a regular basis.

- **Step Two: Take action on the ideas that can be easily implemented.** There was one client we had, a manager who was spending $7,500 a year for a social media company to manage their Facebook and other social media sites. However, the manager wasn't receiving any enquiries.

  We had a look at what was going on and identified the problem. It was because the page wasn't set up correctly, and there weren't any links to their website, also known as the marketing funnel, so people would just leave after reading their nice post. We had them change to a different company at half the cost, set up the marketing funnel correctly and now the managers have a zero-day vacancy rate while saving $3,500 a year.

- **Step Three: Look at the complex/building from your customers' and tenants' point of view.**
  Recall and record all the feedback your customers and tenants gave you when you did your open inspections. Also, look at your competitors' buildings and online advertising. Understand and list the reasons why tenants/customers might choose their buildings over yours, and discuss the items on your list with your owners and committee members. There will be new projects to

improve your building, and you may get paid more to carry out extra work if the tasks aren't within the scope of your agreements or their expectations of you as the building manager.

Please contact SIRE if you would like to see real-life case studies or need assistance.

- **Step Four: Look at your building from your investors' point of view.**
All investors want to get as much rent as possible, but some properties managed by outside agents may not know you or the superior services you provide if they don't live on-site.

For example, they might not realise you get higher rent rates than outside agents, so you're in the best position to recommend areas that require refurbishment. If there's something in the common areas that needs replacing/repair/upgrading, then you should check the Sinking Fund Forecast (SFF), and see if there's money allocated for these improvements.

If there are no allocations for expenditure in the SFF, you will need to discuss the issue with the committee and arrange for a quantity surveyor to come out and prepare a customised SFF for your building. Once this is completed, the expenditures can be allocated in the next financial year's budget.

If items inside the units require replacing, you will need to discuss this directly with the owner. Sometimes they don't want to spend any money on their unit, so you need to adjust the rent rate accordingly to compete with the market. Sometimes the owner does want to spend money on improving their apartment, and you can upgrade it when it becomes vacant. Or maybe the owner does want to upgrade, but they don't have enough cash to do it straight away. This is where you can use the strategy of withholding a portion of the weekly rent that you and the owner agree upon and deposit it into your trust account, so when the tenant vacates the property, the upgrade can be completed.

Once you've done your assessment and made the improvements, adjust your rent accordingly. There are service providers who can assist you with this process. Contact the SIRE Team for more details.

- **Step Five: Investigate all marketing and sales options.**
Many companies use social media to acquire a fortune in the accommodation industry. Make a list of all marketing ideas you could implement to increase interest in your complex.

For example, one short-term accommodation provider made the pool area into the most Instagrammable place during that year, so lots of guests would take photos and post them on Instagram. People would see the photos and want to come and share the experience.

- **Step Six: Systemise and document your daily duties.**
Build step-by-step systems for tasks that are repetitive, and then outsource them to contractors.

- **Step Seven: Utilise the latest technology.**
Update the technology you're using, so you become more efficient and productive. Investigate the latest tools, equipment, machines,

software, hardware and apps that will help you get your work done in half the time.

## What are the most frequently asked questions you receive from managers trying to improve their business?

As you begin your journey to improve your business, you may encounter a few roadblocks along the way. Let me make the process easier for you by answering the top three most frequently asked questions we receive:

- **What if I'm busy and don't have time to do all of these steps?**
  Just remember that when people say they're busy, it's not necessarily true that they're working on dollar-producing tasks. There was this one manager who told me he was "very business-oriented", but after spending an hour observing him going about his day, I discovered that he just loved chatting with everyone in the building.

  I pointed out that while it was great that he stayed in communication with the residents, his conversations could be more to the point, and they would be just as happy, especially if he provided them with a quick and effective solution.

  So "busyness" can be an illusion. I used to have this illusion myself, and it took almost a year for me to overcome it. If you have a hard time streamlining your tasks, get someone with more experience or a coach to help you.

  While you may think you don't have time to systemise a reoccurring task, all it requires is a mindset shift. Ask yourself if it's worth to take an extra thirty minutes just one time to systemise this task that will save you ten minutes every day, or 60.8 hours every year. If you look at it that way, you'll begin to understand how it's a pretty good return on your investment and worth the effort.

- **What if my body corporate or owner doesn't want to spend the money?**
This really depends on how you present your idea to the owners/investors. Your first priority is to provide feedback to make them aware of what's happening. Before going to the owners, get three quotes, so you can tell them exactly how much everything will cost, as well as the return they'll get on their investment, such as higher rent for investors and a better property value for the owners.

Another strategy to complete a project, or at least get one started, is to break it down into modules, where each one is a key milestone. Every module therefore costs less than the entire project, and you can work within your expenditure boundary and limited funds.

Of course, there's also the satisfaction of walking through the complex and feeling great because of how much you've improved it, or at least gotten the ball rolling. This project module approach works quite well, because the residents actually see things getting improved over time and become generally supportive of your goals.

Depending on your spending limits as the building manager, you may be able to simply approve the quote. But if the cost exceeds your expenditure limit, you need the majority of the committee to approve it. Or if the cost exceeds the committee's expenditure limit, the motion should be submitted for a general meeting, and everyone needs to agree to it.

If the body corporate doesn't have the funds to proceed with the project, you'll need to ensure there are provisions allocating funding in the following financial year's budget. At least you've proven that you know what to do, and the owners will get an understanding of what you want, so when the funds do come in, you'll be ready. Most of the time, you can get extra pay if this service isn't in your caretaking agreement. It's just another way to increase your income! Contact the SIRE Team if you need assistance.

- **What if I don't have the knowledge to do some of these steps?**
  There are many service providers who can help you. At SIRE, we've implemented most of these strategies ourselves and developed simple steps for you to follow, along with valuable and reliable contacts that can help you.

In summary, here are the steps you need to implement:

1. Set aside forty-five minutes to go through your profit-and-loss statement.
2. Brainstorm your ideas, and write them down as they come to you.
3. Implement one idea per week from the easiest to the hardest.

By following these steps, within three months you'll have a great business, as well as more income and time.

If you need assistance, just contact SIRE to join our monthly workshops, so you'll be able to set three small action plans that will improve the value of your management rights.

## What are the best ways for someone to market their business to their owners, prospective tenants and guests?

I like to say, "The riches are in the niches". On-site managers are in a niche sector, and they have many unique advantages compared to outside agents, such as achieving higher rent rates, lower vacancy rates and being able to perform more inspections at times that are convenient for the prospective clients.

But some managers are in a better position to recognise and market these advantages to their owners and residents than others. Once they're identified, managers can systemise their marketing funnels and use the latest technologies to target their prospective clients as identified by following these three simple steps:

1. **Create lead magnets with promotional offers that are attractive for the prospective clients.**
   You can use market funnels like social media, email, text messaging, phone calling, your website and portal advertising.

2. **Add value to your prospective clients on a regular basis.**
   Creating content that's relevant to your clients' interests, such as special events in the area for guests and residents, or tax benefits for owners with property and fixture depreciation that will increase their after-tax income. These value-adding ideas are promoted to your current and prospective clients using your marketing funnels.

3. **Identify their issues, and offer them your services.**
   For instance, some owners may have their unit vacant for some time, and you can offer them your letting service with a professional

photography rebate after you've leased the unit. Once again, these services are promoted using your marketing funnels.

Just remember the rule about fair exchange: only charge the fair amount for the value delivered.

At SIRE, we have a panel of experts who can assist you with improving your productivity.

> *There is no greater reward than working from your heart, and making a difference in the world.*
> ~**Carlos Santana**

**How can someone keep ahead of other operators?**
More and more smaller management rights owners are thinking like big businesses. The following are the four areas in which you need to take action and continually work on:

1. Always work to improve the quality and value of the products and services offered to the clients.

2. Make sure investor owners know about your positive contributions, such as building improvements, renovations and the higher returns you get for your clients.

3. Create an automated client capturing and marketing system, steadily build your database of investor owners and craft and promote attention-

grabbing messages that your investors will share on their social media networks.

4. Automate your marketing by creating a database of your most valuable clients, and then figure out ways of improving their assets and helping them when they need it.

Although this sounds like a lot of work, it will all pay off in the end. If you follow these steps, you'll increase your chance to attract investors.

The typical profile of a building will have some units that are owned by investors, but they're using outside agents for letting and sales services. There's always:

- 3 percent of owners who are actively shopping for a different agent
- 67 percent of owners who are interested in your agency services
- 30 percent that don't want your services.

Your marketing effort should concentrate on the 70 percent who are interested in your services and those who are actively shopping for a different agent. Once the trust is built and they become the 3 percent, you'll get their business. It's that simple.

## What do you believe separates the successful business owner from the rest?

There are key differences between a good manager and a mediocre manager such as attitude, an understanding of human nature, organisational skills and interpersonal skills.

Most importantly, a good manager thinks and acts positively, always maintaining a healthy and happy mindset. They live by the motto that the more you give, the more you receive. I'm not talking about being a charity. It's about providing the best value for your clients to the point where they couldn't possibly get a better deal elsewhere, and they'd be mad not to choose you over the others.

One example of adding more value to the body corporate is to negotiate better prices from the contractors by establishing a personal relationship with them, as well as doing some bulk buying to get a quality job done for less than a third of the price. The owners will notice the good-quality works being done without high levies, and that's the key to winning their trust.

**What do owners really appreciate about their caretaker/ property manager?**
Problem-solving is the key here. Basically, it's about getting good-quality work completed for the best price.

Management rights owners are in the best position to solve problems and deliver the best value. Here are a few reasons:

1. They only focus on one or a few buildings/complexes at a time.

2. They generally pay levies, as do all the other owners, so they have the common interest of saving the body corporate money.

3. They own the letting and caretaking agreements for the building, and the residents frequently interact with them and get to know them, so it's in their best interest to maintain the building's value.

Managers should work on offering a better value to their clients, which is exactly why management rights is such a stable business. The price of supplying the same service compared to an outside agent or company is more cost effective, because on-site managers eliminate the middle man, and they hunt for the 'best bang for the dollar'.

**What one action can people take right now to improve their management rights business?**

By focusing on these six simple steps for the next ninety days, you'll improve your efficiency.

- **Step One: List all the caretaking duties and letting activities that use up your time.**

    These can include:
    - cutting grass
    - mopping the common foyer
    - paperwork
    - routine inspections
    - meeting with committees
    - getting quotes
    - phone calls
    - meetings.

    Include everything, even five-minute tasks. Be specific, clear and brief. Keep going until you've listed everything you can think of.

    1. _____

    2. _____

3.
___

4.
___

5.
___

6.
___

- Step Two: List three tasks you're proficient at and enjoy the most in your management rights business.

    1.
    ___

    2.
    ___

    3.
    ___

- Step Three: List the three most important activities you do that produce income for your management rights business, and put your ninety-day plan in place to focus on it daily.

    1.
    ___

    2.
    ___

    3.
    ___

- **Step Four: Name the three most important activities in which you're not proficient and don't enjoy.**

  1. _____

  2. _____

  3. _____

- **Step Five: List who you could delegate these tasks to, or contact the SIRE Team to assist you with developing your skills.**

  1. _____

  2. _____

  3. _____

- **Step Six: What's the one time-consuming activity you're going to say "No" to right away, and what benefit will result from delegating it?**

  1. _____

  2. _____

  3. _____

We run a Productive Managers Workshop once a year. Go to **www.mrformula.com.au** for more information.

**Do you have any final words you'd like to share?**
Don't go for the broker who offers you the lowest commission. Let's be real here: if they can't negotiate on their own commission, what hope do you have of them negotiating the highest price for your management rights business? Negotiation skills are critical in getting you the highest price, while also ensuring the contract goes all the way to settlement.

Be clear on your desired outcome, and remain upfront with your broker. It gives them the opportunity to reciprocate and promotes a positive and productive working relationship.

## The seven wisdoms from this chapter:

1. Sharing ideas, learning and belonging to a like-minded group of managers is a sure-fire way to build and maintain a valuable management rights business and enjoy the unique lifestyle it provides.

2. Help your clients by making decisions that improve their lives.

3. Your best backups are a great system and the SIRE Team.

4. Price is what you pay, and value is what you get, so always ensure you offer more value to your clients than what you charge.

5. The riches are in the niches.

6. Focus on only three things at one time when you're working on increasing your income

7. To get results, have a team around you that will hold you accountable to finish what you started.

> *If you think education is expensive. Try estimating the cost of ignorance.*
> **~Howard Gardner**

# FREE GIFT

Richard and The SIRE Team have offered readers of *The Management Rights Formula* the option of a special gift of your choosing.

**Option One:**

A FREE health check-up consultation for your management rights team. This is a savings of $2,500. Plus, any reader who decides to sell their management rights and mentions this book, will receive a COMPLIMENTARY advertising upgrade from our standard silver package to our GOLD premier advertising package, an additional saving of more than $1,500.

**Option Two:**

You'll receive a free ticket for our workshop, *Twelve Ways to Improve Your Management Rights*, which includes action plans and the resources to implement them.

To access these great gifts, please visit **www.mrformula.com.au/bonus**.

# HOW TO CLAIM YOUR FREE BONUS GIFTS

Our contributors have generously offered FREE gifts to all of our readers. Here are some of the special bonuses you'll receive simply by visiting our website:

## Free Gift # 1: Let's Buy Management Rights: A Simplified Science

**(Valued at $397.00)**

Sire Management Rights is offering an extraordinary opportunity to participate in our exclusive three-hour workshop, entitled *Apply the Management Rights Formula*, where some of the most successful insiders share everything you need to know about acquiring an excellent management rights, so you can live the lifestyle you deserve.

**You'll learn their strategies, processes, systems and procedures for building better relationships** with owners and improving the products and services you provide to the market, so you can deliver the performance your owners will rave about. Go to **www.mrformula.com.au/bonus** to start your adventure today.

## Free Gift # 2: The Winning Formula: The 3E's

**(Valued at over $1,500)**

Danny Little is offering readers of *The Management Rights Formula* a complete, tailor-made operations manual for your first building purchase. This manual will:

- improve your efficiency and save time
- ensure services are delivered consistently
- save you 60 percent in training costs when you recruit a new staff or relief manager.

**You can have it for FREE!**
To access this awesome gift, please visit **www.mrformula.com.au/bonus**.

## Free Gift # 3: Show Me the Money: What You Need To Know to Succeed

**(Valued at $550.00)**

Jason Fu is offering readers of *The Management Rights Formula* a free complete, tailor-made VIP financial review consultation.

This will save you significant time, as he'll only present management rights within your price range and will help you set up the correct loan structure for tax savings and expanding your portfolio.

To claim this amazing gift, visit **www.mrformula.com.au/bonus**.

## Free Gift # 4: Break Through Your First Million, Systemise, Build a Team and Increase Your Profit

(Valued at $99.00)

Michael O'Farrell is offering readers a free webinar on the step-by-step guide to attracting and retaining talent.

If you're a manager who wants to grow and scale your business, and have a multi-million-dollar yearly net income, please go to **www.mrformula.com.au/bonus** to join the webinar.

## Free Gift # 5: Turbocharge Your Profit: Make Your Technology Work for You

(Valued at $297.00)

Sylvia Johnston is offering readers of *The Management Rights Formula* a free website assessment for those who want to get more direct bookings, increase their occupancy rate and receive a website improvement formula.

To claim your awesome gift, visit **www.mrformula.com.au/bonus**.

## Free Gift # 6: Prevent Forest Fires: Strategic Legal Advice From Business–Minded Lawyers

(A $250.00 value)

John Mahoney has generously offered the readers of *The Management Rights Formula* a free thirty-minute initial consultation on any management rights or body corporate matter. Get your bonus by registering now via **www.mrformula.com.au/bonus**.

## Free Gift # 7: Keep What You Make: Asset Protection and Smart Tax Strategies

**(Valued at $395.00)**

Scott Lai is providing the readers of *The Management Rights Formula* a great bonus consultation session that will help you set up the correct structure to protect your assets and legally save you from paying excessive taxes. With the tools and processes provided in this consultation session, you can save millions.

To claim your awesome gift, visit **www.mrformula.com.au/bonus**.

## Free Gift # 8: Management Rights Super Exit Strategy

**The fast and Simple Way to Sell Your Business at the Highest Price**

The SIRE Team is offering readers of *The Management Rights Formula* a special gift of your choosing.

**Option One:**
A FREE health check-up consultation for your management rights team. This is a savings of $2,500. Plus, any reader who decides to sell their management rights and mentions this book, will receive a COMPLIMENTARY advertising upgrade from our standard silver package to our GOLD premier advertising package, an additional saving of more than $1,500.

**Option Two:**

You'll receive a free ticket for our workshop, *Twelve Ways to Improve Your Management Rights*, which includes action plans and the resources to implement them.

To access these great gifts, please visit **www.mrformula.com.au/bonus**.

Here's a list of even more specialists who can help you on your management rights journey:

For more information about getting your resident letting agent licence, full real estate agent licence and sales and property management certificate, please contact:

**Jason Yang**
Academic Director
**Web:** www.niet.edu.au
**Phone:** 07 3117 1772
**Email:** academic@niet.edu.au
**Address:** 7 & 8 Clunies Ross Court, Eight Mile Plains Q4113
**RTO:** 41422 | **CRICOS:** 03590D

**Management Rights Insurance Brokers**

**Ben Liu**—Director
**M :** 0404 155 555
**F :** 07 3278 2339
**E :** ben@redbroking.com
**W :** www.redbroking.com
Suite 1, 250 Sherwood Road, Rocklea Qld 4106

**Amax Cleaning**

**Max CHang**
Manager
**Web:** www.amaxcleaning.com.au
**Phone:** 0459576666
**Email:** admin@amaxcleaning.com.au
**Address:** unit 1/19 Aberdeen Cres, Kuraby QLD 4112

---

To access your free bonus gifts, go to **www.mrformula.com.au/bonus**, and follow the instructions.

www.ingramcontent.com/pod-product-compliance
Lightning Source LLC
Chambersburg PA
CBHW082249300426

44110CB00039B/2492